ÁSATRÚ

THE HEATHEN PATH

A Beginner's Guide to Modern
Paganism | Revive the Spiritual
Legacy of Norse Gods

ERIK HANSEN

For permission requests, please contact:
Novus Liber Publishing
Email: info@yourbookshelf.top

First edition October 2024
Revised edition March 2026

eBook ISBN 978-1-961963-26-9
Paperback ISBN 978-1-961963-27-6

"There is no man so good that he has no flaw, nor a man so bad he's good for nothing."

— *Hávamál, st. 133*

Contents

Introduction

The gods of the Norse tradition have been dead for a thousand years. That, at least, is the official story.

The actual story is more interesting. Across Europe and North America, tens of thousands of people are practicing a living form of pre-Christian Norse religion—making offerings to Odin and Thor, observing the solstices, honoring their ancestors at seasonal feasts, and building communities organized around values that the Viking Age would have recognized immediately: honor, loyalty, courage, hospitality, and the refusal to let someone else define the terms of your spiritual life. The movement is growing faster than almost any other religious tradition in the Western world. Iceland's national Asatru organization is now the largest non-Christian faith in the country, and recently broke ground on the first major Norse temple since the Viking Age.

This is not a Renaissance fair. It is not white nationalism with a Viking aesthetic—a contamination that serious practitioners reject explicitly and that has no basis in the actual historical tradition. It is not a game, a subculture, or a nostalgic fantasy. It is a reconstruction of an ancient polytheistic religion, undertaken with scholarly seriousness and real spiritual commitment, by people who find in it something they could not find elsewhere.

What they find, typically, is this: a faith that locates the sacred in practice rather than in belief, that asks what you *do* rather than what you *profess*, that holds you accountable to your community rather than to an invisible judge, and that treats the natural world as inhabited and worthy of attention rather

1

than as a backdrop to the human drama. A faith, also, that is honest about difficulty—that does not promise salvation or comfort of the easy kind, but offers instead a framework for meeting whatever comes with your eyes open and your values intact.

Asatru has no pope, no single sacred text, no central authority, and no interest in converting anyone. It seeks no one. People find it—usually as adults, usually after a long period of looking for something they could not quite name—and they choose it deliberately, with full awareness of what they are taking on. That structure shapes everything about how the tradition works.

This book is a complete introduction to that tradition. It covers the history and the revival, the cosmology and the myths, the gods and the beings who share the Norse cosmos, the ethics, the magic, the sacred calendar, and the practical details of building a personal practice—from your first altar to your first blót to your first reading of the Hávamál. It is written for the person who is seriously curious: who wants to understand what Asatru actually is, stripped of both the Hollywood version and the academic one, presented clearly enough to decide whether it is a path worth walking.

One clarification before we begin. Throughout this book, I use the English form *Asatru*—one of several accepted spellings of the tradition's name. The people who practice it call themselves Asatruar, or simply Heathens. Both names have been worn as badges of identity for fifty years now, reclaimed from the contempt with which Christian missionaries originally applied them.

The Old Ways have been waiting a long time. They are not difficult to find.

Chapter 1

The Old Way

A satru is a modern name for an ancient faith. The word comes from Old Norse: áss, meaning "god," and trú, meaning "belief" or "trust"—faith in the gods, specifically the Norse deities known as the Æsir. It is also called Heathenry, Forn Sed, Germanic Neopaganism, or Odinism, depending on who is speaking and which aspect of the tradition they want to emphasize. None of these names is wrong. None is complete.

In the Viking Age, the people who practiced this religion had no special word for it. It was simply the way things were—how you honored the gods, acknowledged the spirits of the land, kept faith with your kin, and understood your place in the world. Only when Christianity began its spread through Northern Europe did the old practitioners need a name for their path at all. They called it Forn Sidr: the Old Way. The name itself tells you something. It was coined in contrast, by people who knew something was being lost.

What exactly was being lost—and how much of it survived—is a question this book takes seriously.

The Shape of the Faith

Asatru is polytheistic. It honors many gods and goddesses, each distinct in character and domain, none of them omnipotent, none of them demanding exclusive devotion. Thor, the Thunderer, wields his hammer Mjölnir and brings the rain that feeds the crops. Odin, the Allfather, gave an eye for wisdom and hung nine days on the World Tree to win the secrets of the runes. Freyja, the most celebrated of the goddesses, rides in a chariot drawn by cats, claims half of those slain in battle, and taught Odin his most powerful magic. Freyr presides over peace, fertility, and the warmth that makes things grow. Behind them stands a full pantheon—Frigg, Tyr, Baldr, Skadi, Heimdallr, and many others—each with their own stories, their own demands, their own relationship to the people who call on them.

Asatru is not only concerned with gods. Practitioners also honor the Landvættir—the land spirits bound to trees, rivers, rocks, and the living earth—and the ancestors, the dead who remain connected to their descendants across the boundary between worlds. The Norse cosmos was understood as inhabited at every level, and that understanding shapes the tradition's approach to everything from daily ritual to the choice of where to build a house.

What holds this together is not a creed. There is no Asatru equivalent of the Apostles' Creed, no set of propositions you are required to affirm. The tradition's ethical core is expressed instead through action and through a set of values—courage, honesty, fidelity, honor, discipline, hospitality, industriousness, self-reliance, perseverance—that the modern revival has formalized as the Nine Noble Virtues. These are not commandments handed down from above. They are a distillation of what the myths and the sagas consistently reward: a person who shows up, keeps their word, and contributes something of worth to the people around them.

Two things distinguish Asatru from the Abrahamic traditions with which most Western readers are more familiar. The first is the absence of any concept of original sin. Human beings are not fallen creatures in need of redemption. They are participants in a living cosmos, capable of honor or dishonor, with the consequences of their choices rippling outward through their communities and forward through time. The second is the near-total absence of missionary impulse. Norse religion spread historically through contact and cultural absorption—when the Norse settled in new lands, they tended to incorporate local beliefs rather than displace them. The tradition has no interest in converting anyone. It asks only that those who come to it come in earnest.

Roots

Asatru's origins stretch back roughly four thousand years, to the Bronze Age cultures of Northern Europe. From that period through the Viking Age—the eighth to eleventh centuries—a recognizable tradition evolved across Scandinavia, the British Isles, Iceland, and the Germanic mainland, expressed in shared myths, seasonal rituals, and a common understanding of the cosmos. It was never a single unified religion with a central authority. It was a family of related practices, varying by region and community, held together by shared stories and shared gods.

The formal end of this world came in stages, but the sharpest moment of rupture occurred in Iceland around the year 1000. The Althing—the Icelandic commonwealth parliament, one of the earliest legislative assemblies in the world—officially declared the country Christian. The decision was driven less by conviction than by political pressure: Christian Europe controlled trade routes Iceland could not afford to lose. The compromise struck was, by the standards of the age, relatively measured. Public pagan practice was prohibited; private practice was initially permitted. Within a generation or two, outward observance of the old religion had effectively disappeared.

What did not disappear were the stories. Iceland remained a culture of poets and historians, and the myths, sagas, and skaldic verses of the Norse world were written down rather than destroyed—preserved in manuscripts that would survive to become the primary sources for everything the modern tradition knows about the pre-Christian past. The Poetic Edda, the Prose Edda, the Icelandic sagas: none of these would exist in the form we have them without the Christian scholars who committed them to parchment, a fact that shapes how they must be read. What the conversion ended was public practice, not memory. The tradition went underground—into folk custom, into poetry, into the kind of knowledge that grandparents pass to grandchildren in stories that no longer announce their religious content. It waited.

Why Now

People come to Asatru for many reasons, but a pattern runs through most of their accounts. They were looking for a spiritual framework that took the world seriously—as the actual terrain of a human life, worth engaging with on its own terms rather than as a staging ground for salvation or something to be transcended. They wanted a tradition that located the sacred in what you do rather than in what you believe, that held the community together through obligation and practice rather than shared doctrine, and that was honest about the difficulty of living well without offering false comfort in return.

What they found in Asatru was a faith built around exactly those priorities. The Norse tradition has no concept of grace—no mechanism by which an outside force resolves the consequences of your choices. What you do accumulates. The deeds of a life become, at death, a permanent feature of the web of wyrd, shaping the possibilities available to those who come after you. This is a clarifying vision rather than a punishing one. It means that how you live matters in a way that is concrete, traceable, and impossible to outsource.

There is also the matter of the natural world. Pre-Christian Norse religion was practiced by people whose survival depended on an intimate understanding of seasonal rhythms, weather, soil, and sea. That intimacy shaped the tradition at every level—the calendar of holy tides aligned to the solstices and equinoxes, the offerings made to the land spirits before plowing a field, the understanding that the dead remained present in the land they had worked. For practitioners living in a world increasingly abstracted from those rhythms, the tradition offers something rare: a framework for paying attention to the physical world as something sacred rather than merely useful.

None of this requires believing in the Norse gods in any literal sense, though many practitioners do. What it requires is a willingness to engage with the tradition's practices seriously—to show up, make the offerings, observe the seasons, maintain the relationships. The gods, in this framework, are approached as presences whose reality is demonstrated through practice rather than established by argument. You do not need to resolve the theological question before you begin. You begin, and the question becomes less urgent over time.

A Faith of Choice

Almost no one is born into Asatru. In Christianity, Islam, and Judaism, the overwhelming majority of practitioners were raised in the faith from childhood. Asatru, by contrast, is built almost entirely from people who found it as adults—who came through curiosity, or a feeling of recognition, or a long dissatisfaction with the spiritual options available to them, and who chose it deliberately, after reflection. This makes it, in a structural sense, a religion of free will. Its practitioners cannot claim the faith by inheritance. They have to make an argument for it, at least to themselves, and keep making it with each passing year.

That is not a weakness. For a tradition that prizes honesty and self-reliance as core virtues, there is something fitting about the fact that no one arrives at it without deciding to. The path is not handed to you. You find it, you assess it, and you choose to walk it—or you don't. The tradition will not pursue you.

What this book offers is the clearest possible picture of what you would be choosing. The chapters that follow cover the cosmology that gives Asatru its shape, the primary texts that preserve its mythology, the gods and other beings that populate its world, the values that structure its ethics, the magical practices at its core, the symbols that carry its meaning, the rituals through which it is lived, the calendar that organizes its year, and the tradition's understanding of death and what follows it. The final chapter addresses the practical question of how to begin.

By the end, you will know what Asatru is. Whether it is yours to walk is a question only you can answer.

Chapter 2

The Revival

Odin and Thor are still going strong, a thousand years after the Viking Age ended. The old Nordic faith never truly vanished with the arrival of Christianity—it retreated, practiced quietly, preserved in poetry and folk custom and the stories that grandparents told children long after the churches had been built. What is happening now is not so much a survival as a conscious revival: a deliberate return to something that was waiting to be found again.

Modern Asatru is practiced openly across the globe—in Sweden, Denmark, Norway, Germany, the United Kingdom, the Netherlands, North America, and Australia, with smaller communities in dozens of other countries. Its spiritual heartland remains Iceland, where the tradition has achieved a visibility and legal recognition unmatched anywhere else in the world. But the shape of the faith, and the questions it grapples with, are shaped by the full complexity of the twenty-first century. Understanding modern Asatru means understanding not just what practitioners believe and do, but the social and cultural currents in which the tradition is swimming.

Iceland: The Living Center

The story of modern Asatru begins in Iceland on the first day of summer, 1972, when Sveinbjörn Beinteinsson—a farmer, poet, and keeper of the old oral traditions—joined with eleven others to formally re-establish public worship of the Norse gods. The government recognized Ásatrúarfélagið as an official religious organization in 1973, granting it the same legal standing as the Lutheran church that had dominated Icelandic religious life for centuries.

At its founding, the organization had fewer than a hundred members and almost no resources. For most of its early period membership did not exceed a hundred people, and after the initial enthusiasm of the founding years faded, there was relatively little activity. What changed everything was patience, cultural shift, and the slow accumulation of people who found that the old ways resonated with something they were looking for and not finding elsewhere.

According to Statistics Iceland, there are now 5,435 registered members in Ásatrúarfélagið, making it the largest non-Christian faith in Iceland. The growth trajectory is striking: membership has grown by more than 240% since 2007, making Asatru the fastest-growing religion in Iceland over the past two decades. Meanwhile, the National Church—once attended by 89% of Icelanders at the start of this century—has fallen to 65.6% of the population, a decline that shows no sign of reversing.

The most visible symbol of this growth is the hof under construction on the southern slope of Öskjuhlíð hill in Reykjavík—Iceland's first major temple to the Norse gods since the Viking Age. The project has had a complicated history: development began in 2005, was delayed repeatedly by the 2008–2011 Icelandic financial crisis and technical problems with the design, and finally broke ground at the solar eclipse of 20 March 2015. By 2022, the administrative offices were functional, with the primary ceremonial and social halls still incomplete. As of 2024, the building hosts ongoing activities in its completed sections, with the second phase—encompassing expanded social facilities, a library, café, and feast halls—slated for completion in 2026.

The hof's design reflects the tradition's values directly: a south-facing glass wall that tracks the sun's movement, a domed ceiling with a skylight, and local stone and timber throughout. It is built to be open to the wider community—conceived not as an exclusive religious space but as a cultural and spiritual center for all of Reykjavík.

Ásatrúarfélagið is led by an allsherjargoði—a chief priest—and currently counts among its goðar both men and women in roughly equal numbers. It is legally authorized to officiate at marriages, naming ceremonies, and funerals. It has protested Iceland's largest dam project on environmental grounds—the only religious organization in Iceland to do so. In 2014, it issued a formal statement against the use of its name and tradition to promote supremacist ideology, militarism, or animal sacrifice. It has consistently positioned itself as a religion of tolerance, ecological responsibility, and democratic organization—values that are not incidental to the faith but rooted in its understanding of the relationship between humans, the land, and the divine.

A Global Community

Beyond Iceland, Asatru takes different forms in different contexts, shaped by local culture, history, and the particular questions each community brings to the tradition.

In Scandinavia, organized Heathen communities exist in Denmark, Sweden, and Norway, each with their own national organizations and their own relationships to the folk traditions and historical sources most directly relevant to their region. Denmark's Forn Siðr organization has achieved legal recognition and officiates at civil ceremonies. Norwegian and Swedish groups vary in their approaches from close reconstructionism to more eclectic practice.

In Germany, the connection to the Germanic pre-Christian tradition runs alongside an uncomfortable historical legacy: the appropriation of Norse and Germanic symbols by National Socialism in the twentieth century has left modern German Heathenry with a particular responsibility to distinguish clearly between authentic practice and the political distortions that used the tradition's imagery for their own purposes. German Heathen communities have generally been vigorous in asserting that distinction.

In the United Kingdom, a long tradition of engagement with Norse and Anglo-Saxon heritage feeds a Heathen community that includes some of the movement's most important scholarly voices. The Pagan Federation provides an umbrella structure, and various independent kindreds offer different approaches to the tradition.

In North America, Heathenry is more demographically and organizationally diverse than anywhere else. The continent's size means communities range from large national organizations with hundreds of members to solitary practitioners who may never meet another Heathen in person. The Troth—explicitly inclusive and non-folkish—and the Asatru Folk Assembly—folkish in orientation—are the two largest organizations, and the distance between their positions reflects a live and ongoing debate within American Heathenry about the nature and boundaries of the tradition.

In 2017, the United States Department of Defense officially recognized Asatru and Heathenry, granting adherents full religious freedom across all branches of the military—a landmark moment for a tradition that had long sought institutional recognition alongside more established faiths.

Popular Culture and Its Discontents

The surge in interest in Asatru over the past fifteen years cannot be understood without acknowledging the role of popular culture. Television series like *Vikings* and *The Last Kingdom*, films drawing on Norse mythology, video games set in Norse worlds, and the global reach of the Marvel Cinematic Universe's Thor—all of this has introduced hundreds of millions of people to the surface of the tradition, generating interest that some of them have pursued into something deeper and more serious.

For the Heathen community, this visibility is a decidedly mixed blessing. On one hand, it has brought people to the tradition who might never have found it otherwise—people who began with a casual interest in Norse mythology and discovered, through honest inquiry, a living spiritual path that resonated with something they had been carrying without a name. Practitioners who came through popular culture and then did the work of engaging seriously with the primary sources are no less Heathen for it.

On the other hand, popular culture's version of the Norse tradition is filtered through the requirements of dramatic entertainment and the assumptions of a broadly Christian-shaped Western audience. The gods are simplified into archetypes. The ethical complexity of the mythology is flattened. The relationship between human and divine—which in the actual tradition is one of reciprocity rather than the worship of a superhero—is distorted almost beyond recognition. The goðar of Ásatrúarfélagið note wryly that explaining what Asatru actually is to someone whose primary reference point is Marvel's Thor requires more patience than explaining it to someone who came with no prior exposure at all.

The serious practitioner learns to hold these two things simultaneously: gratitude for the curiosity that popular culture generates, and the responsibility to offer something more substantial when that curiosity arrives.

The Digital Community

Modern Asatru has also been transformed by the internet in ways that would have been impossible to anticipate when the revival began in the 1970s. Online communities—forums, social media groups, Discord servers, YouTube channels, and podcasts—have created a global conversation among practitioners that crosses the geographic isolation that previously made solitary practice deeply lonely.

For many practitioners, particularly those without access to a local kindred, online community provides essential connection: a space to ask questions, share practice, argue about the lore, and develop a sense of belonging to something larger than individual solitary work. The quality of these communities varies enormously—from rigorous scholarly discussion to the perpetuation of serious misunderstandings—but their existence has fundamentally changed the landscape of who can access the tradition and how.

The digital environment has also accelerated the spread of both good information and bad. Accurate accounts of Norse history and religion coexist online with romanticized distortions, conspiracy theories, and the deliberate appropriation of Heathen imagery by extremist groups who have learned that social media platforms are effective vectors for their messaging. Navigating this environment requires the same critical discernment that the tradition itself cultivates: a commitment to working with primary sources, a healthy skepticism toward claims not grounded in actual scholarship, and the intellectual honesty to distinguish between what the lore says and what someone wants it to say.

The Folkish Question

No account of modern Asatru can avoid the most significant internal debate the tradition faces: the question of whether Heathenry is a universal spiritual path, open to anyone who seriously engages with it, or a folk religion tied to ethnic heritage and therefore appropriately restricted to people of Northern European descent.

The so-called "folkish" position—that Asatru is the indigenous spiritual tradition of people of Germanic ancestry and that ethnic background is relevant to practice—has been part of the Heathen movement since its early days, and organizations holding this view continue to exist and attract members. The opposing "universalist" position holds that the tradition is defined by cultural and spiritual engagement rather than biology, and that restricting it along ethnic lines has no historical basis in how Norse religion actually functioned and represents a contamination of the tradition with modern racial ideology.

The historical evidence strongly supports the universalist position. Norse paganism spread across a vast geographic area through trade, migration, and cultural contact, and was practiced by people of diverse ethnic backgrounds across the Viking Age world. The tradition defined its insiders by participation in its practices and acceptance of its values, not by bloodline. The deliberate association of Norse imagery with white identity politics is a product of nineteenth-century German nationalism and twentieth-century fascism—not of the pre-Christian Norse world.

Ásatrúarfélagið has been explicit on this point, issuing a formal statement that it strongly opposes any attempt to use the Ásatrú name to promote supremacist ideology, militarism, or animal sacrifice. The Troth, one of the largest American Heathen organizations, is similarly explicit in its commitment to inclusivity. Many other organizations and independent kindreds across the English-speaking world have issued formal statements rejecting folkish positions.

The practical consequence for newcomers is simple: when researching community affiliation, pay attention to how organizations discuss this question. A group that restricts membership by ethnic background is practicing something that departs significantly from the tradition's historical character. The gods of the Norse tradition were not tribal gods in the narrow ethnic sense—they were cosmic forces whose relationship with humanity was never defined by bloodline alone.

Who Practices Asatru Today

The demographic reality of modern Asatru is considerably more varied than popular representation suggests. While the tradition has historically attracted disproportionate attention from men—particularly through its connection to warrior imagery and Viking aesthetics—contemporary Heathen communities are more evenly distributed across gender than this attention implies.

Women have been central to the Asatru revival from its earliest days. Freyja is among the most widely honored deities, the völva tradition of female shamanic practice has been actively reconstructed by women practitioners, and the dísablót and ancestor veneration practices that are among Asatru's most distinctive features have historically been led by women in the household context. In Iceland, the current leadership of Ásatrúarfélagið includes women in prominent roles, and the organization has officiated at same-sex marriages since before Iceland's civil marriage law required equal treatment.

LGBTQ+ practitioners are present and visible in many Heathen communities, particularly in universalist organizations. The Norse tradition's relationship to gender and sexuality is complicated—it contained both strict gender norms and figures like Loki, whose gender and sexuality transgressed those norms with apparent impunity, and Óðinn, who practiced seiðr despite its association with femininity. This complexity has made the tradition available for queer interpretation in ways that some practitioners find meaningful and others contest.

Reconstructionism and Living Practice

One of the liveliest ongoing conversations in modern Heathenry is the question of how closely contemporary practice should follow the historical record—and what to do in the many areas where that record is fragmentary, ambiguous, or silent.

Strict reconstructionists hold that practice should be grounded as closely as possible in what the primary sources and archaeological evidence actually support, and that innovations not grounded in the lore should be clearly identified as such. This position produces rigorous, historically informed practice but can struggle with the inevitable gaps in the surviving evidence.

At the other end of the spectrum, more eclectic practitioners draw on the Norse tradition alongside other pagan and magical systems, prioritizing living spiritual experience over historical accuracy. This produces a more fluid and personally responsive practice but risks losing contact with what makes Asatru specifically Asatru rather than a generic neo-paganism with Norse aesthetics.

Most practitioners occupy a middle ground—working seriously with the primary sources while acknowledging that a living tradition must breathe, adapt, and find ways to address questions that the historical sources never anticipated. The distinction between lore (what the texts actually say) and UPG (Unverified Personal Gnosis—the insights that come from direct spiritual experience rather than textual grounding) has become a useful practical tool for navigating this tension, allowing communities to maintain intellectual honesty about the basis of their claims while preserving space for the personal and experiential dimensions of practice.

The phrase heard most often in Heathen communities—"Asatru is a spirituality with homework"—captures this orientation exactly. The tradition does not hand you a ready-made faith. It hands you a body of extraordinary material and asks you to do the work of engaging with it seriously, honestly, and for the long term.

Chapter 3

Who Heathens Are

People often ask me: what does it actually mean to be Asatru? Not what to read, or which gods to honor, or how to set up an altar — those questions have their own chapter, near the end of this book. What they want to know is something harder to pin down. What kind of person does this tradition expect you to be?

The short answer is that Asatru has no rules in the doctrinal sense — no catechism, no list of required beliefs, no authority empowered to declare you in or out. What it has instead is a set of expectations, and they run deeper than rules. You are expected to act with honor. You are expected to take responsibility for what you do. You are expected to contribute something of worth to the people around you, and to keep your word when you give it. These are not conditions of membership. They are descriptions of character — the kind of character the tradition has always recognized as its own.

The Norse understood this through the concept of weregild: when you cause harm, you make it right, in a measure at least equal to the damage done. You do not explain it away, minimize it, or wait for someone else to fix it. The obligation is yours, and meeting it is part of what it means to live with honor. This is a tradition that takes human fallibility seriously — the gods themselves make mistakes, as anyone who has read the myths knows — but it has no patience for people who treat their mistakes as someone else's problem.

Honor, in this context, is not a private matter. It exists in relationship — between you and your kindred, between you and the wider community, between you and the gods who are watching not with judgment but with the particular attention of those who have also had to make hard choices under difficult circumstances. The Norse gods are not distant perfections. They are figures of power and complexity who have paid real costs for what they carry. Odin gave an eye. Tyr gave a hand. Freyr gave his sword, and will face Ragnarök without it. What the tradition asks of its practitioners is not worship in the sense of submission, but something closer to the respect you might show a worthy elder — someone whose experience you take seriously and whose example you try to live up to, knowing you will sometimes fall short.

When you fall short, you get back up. That, too, is part of the tradition.

Three Currents

Modern Asatru is not a single unified movement. It is a family of related practices held together by shared sources and shared gods, and it contains genuine disagreements — some of them significant — about who the tradition is for and how it should be practiced.

The most consequential of these disagreements concerns the question of ancestry. Three broad positions have emerged within the Heathen community, and anyone entering the tradition will encounter all three.

Universalists hold that Asatru is open to anyone who engages with it seriously, regardless of ethnic background. The tradition is defined by what you do and how you live — by your relationship to the values, the lore, and the community — not by your bloodline. A practitioner whose ancestors came from Japan, or Nigeria, or anywhere else can be fully Heathen, provided they bring the same commitment and seriousness that the tradition asks of everyone. The main criticism of this position is that it sets few entry conditions beyond sincere interest, which some feel leaves the tradition too diffuse to hold its shape. This criticism is worth hearing, though it should be noted that most universalist organizations expect real engagement — the tradition is not, on any serious account, an invitation to sample casually and move on.

Folkish practitioners take the opposite position: Asatru is an ethnic religion, rooted in the ancestral heritage of Northern European peoples, and it is most authentically practiced by those who share that heritage. Folkish advocates often draw a parallel to Shinto, which is similarly bound to a specific people and their land, and they are generally careful to distinguish their position from white supremacy — a distinction that matters in principle, even if the line is not always clearly maintained in practice.

The historical argument against ethnic exclusivity is straightforward and difficult to counter: Norse religious life throughout the Viking Age was practiced by people of diverse backgrounds. Norse thralls came from Ireland, Poland, the British Isles, and as far as the Middle East; when enslaved people lived in Norse lands, they participated in Norse customs. When the Norse settled elsewhere, they absorbed local practice. The tradition's historical insiders were defined by cultural participation, not bloodline.

Tribalism positions itself as a middle ground. Tribalists generally accept non-white practitioners into their communities, but insist on a demonstrated commitment to Norse culture as a prerequisite — what they describe as a formal adoption into the community, comparable to conversion in Judaism. The analogy is imperfect but not meaningless: there is something to the idea that a living tradition requires more than casual interest to sustain, and that the act of formal commitment changes the nature of one's relationship to the community.

You do not have to choose between these positions immediately, or perhaps ever. What you should do is understand them clearly enough to make an informed decision about which communities you want to be part of — and to recognize that a group restricting membership on racial grounds is practicing something with roots not in pre-Christian Scandinavia, but in nineteenth-century German nationalism and twentieth-century fascism. The historical tradition knew nothing of such restrictions.

On Living Among Non-Heathens

Most people who come to Asatru do not live in exclusively Heathen worlds. They have Christian family members, colleagues who have never heard of Ásatrúarfélagið, neighbors whose religious lives are entirely their own business. Navigating this is something every practitioner works out for themselves, but a few principles hold broadly.

Within a family, the goal is peace — not agreement, but the kind of coexistence that allows relationships to remain intact across genuine difference. Most people follow the faith they were raised in because it is the one they know, and argument is rarely the path to understanding in either direction. The ancestors of modern Asatru were traders and diplomats as well as warriors; they understood that relationships maintained over time are worth more than any single confrontation. Seek common ground where it exists. Keep the peace where you can. Let your life speak for itself rather than trying to explain beliefs that require living context to make sense.

In professional life, the same principle applies with even less room for drama. You are not required to advertise your religion. You are not required to hide it. What you are required to do — by the tradition's own standards — is conduct yourself with honesty and integrity, keep your commitments, and let your reputation be built on what you actually do. The pre-Christian Norse were respected traders across a continent precisely because their word was reliable. That inheritance is available to anyone who chooses to carry it.

Wyrd and Frith

Two concepts from the Norse tradition are worth introducing here, because they shape how Heathens understand their place in the world more than almost anything else.

Wyrd is the force that binds all things across time — the web of consequences that connects every action to its effects, every choice to what it makes possible or forecloses. Modern Heathens understand this not as fatalism but as a form of accountability: who you are today reflects the choices you and others have made in the past, and every decision you make now is already shaping the possibilities available to those who come after you. This understanding runs through the tradition's ethics at every level. If what you do has real consequences that ripple outward through the people connected to you, then taking your actions seriously is not optional. It is the foundational obligation of a Heathen life.

Frith is the preservation of peace and goodwill within a community — the quality of relationship that makes collective life possible. The pre-Christian Norse lived in conditions where the bonds between people were often the difference between survival and its absence, and they took those bonds with corresponding seriousness. Hospitality was not a social grace but a near-sacred obligation: you offered shelter and food to those who came to you in need, because the network of mutual obligation that sustained communities across vast distances depended on everyone holding up their part of it. Gift-giving operated on the same principle — not as transaction, but as the visible expression of a relationship that both parties chose to maintain.

In contemporary Heathen communities, frith looks different in its particulars but rests on the same foundation: showing up, following through, treating the people in your kindred as people whose wellbeing you have taken on as part of your own responsibility. Keeping your word is taken seriously enough that many practitioners will decline to commit to something they are not certain they can deliver — because a broken oath is not simply a social inconvenience. It is a fracture in the web, with consequences that extend further than the immediate disappointment.

Honesty, directness, and the willingness to be accountable — these are not abstract virtues in the Asatru context. They are the daily practice of a person who understands themselves as part of something larger than their individual life, and who has chosen to act accordingly.

Does Ancestry Matter?

According to the Eddas, the first man and woman were shaped from ash and elm. There is no mention of their being white, or Nordic, or anything else that the twentieth century would have found meaningful. Everyone is invited to take part in the effort to maintain the balance between order and chaos that the tradition understands as the central work of human life.

Some who call themselves Asatruar will disagree with that framing. Disagreements of this kind exist in most traditions, and Asatru is not exempt. The answer the tradition's own historical record gives is clear: what made someone Norse was not blood, but practice — the gods they honored, the oaths they kept, the community they belonged to and sustained. That answer is available to anyone willing to take it seriously.

Chapter 4

The Nine Worlds and the Cosmos

B efore you can understand the gods of Asatru, the rituals, or the runes, you need a map. Not of the physical world, but of the Norse cosmos—a living, layered reality that the ancient Heathens believed surrounded and sustained all existence.

Most people encounter Norse mythology through popular culture, where the cosmos is little more than a dark backdrop. For practitioners of Asatru, the structure of the universe is a theological statement. Every blót, every prayer, every act of worship takes place within this framework. Understanding the Nine Worlds is not academic preparation. It is the foundation of everything that follows.

The Norse cosmos is held together by a single great axis: Yggdrasil, the World Tree, an immense ash whose roots reach into the deepest realms and whose branches shelter the highest. Hanging from that tree are nine distinct worlds—each inhabited by its own peoples, its own forces, its own relationship to the divine.

But before there were worlds, before there was even a tree to hold them, there was the void.

Ginnungagap: The Void Before the Beginning

The Norse creation story does not begin with a god speaking light into darkness. It begins with emptiness—and with two opposing forces so far apart they should never have met.

Ginnungagap—the "yawning void"—was not nothingness in the modern sense. It was closer to pure potential: an immense, silent space waiting for the conditions that would force creation into being.

To the north lay Niflheimr, a world of ice, mist, and impenetrable cold. From it flowed eleven rivers whose waters froze as they traveled into the void, filling the northern reaches of Ginnungagap with layer upon layer of poisonous rime. To the south lay Múspellsheimr, a realm of pure fire and chaos, guarded by the giant Surtr. When the ice met the fire, it began to melt—and from the dripping water, two figures emerged.

The first was Ymir, the first living being, neither god nor man. As he slept, other giants were born from his sweat. He was nourished by a massive cow, Auðumbla, who fed by licking the salty ice. In doing so, she uncovered a figure buried within it: on the first day, hair; on the second, a head; on the third, the full form of Búri, ancestor of the gods. Búri's grandson was Óðinn, who together with his brothers Vili and Vé killed Ymir and built the world from his remains. His flesh became the earth, his bones the mountains, his blood the seas. His skull was raised as the dome of the sky. From two trees found on the shore, the brothers fashioned the first man and woman—Askr and Embla—and set them to live in the protected enclosure at the center of creation.

The ground beneath your feet was made from something that once lived—which is why Asatru's reverence for the natural world is not sentiment but theology. To honor the earth is to honor the very substance of creation.

Yggdrasil: The World Tree

Yggdrasil is what holds it all together. The great ash at the center of Norse cosmology is not decorative symbolism—it is, within the Norse understanding of the universe, the structural fact of reality. Remove it, and the Nine Worlds do not simply drift apart. They cease to exist.

The name is most commonly interpreted as "Óðinn's horse"—a kenning rooted in the fact that Óðinn once hung from its branches for nine days and nine nights, pierced by his own spear, in order to receive the knowledge of the runes. In Old Norse tradition, the gallows was called "the horse of the hanged." That the tree bears this name tells you something essential: even the axis of the universe is understood through the lens of sacrifice willingly chosen in pursuit of wisdom.

Three roots extend from its base, each drawing from a different well. The first drinks from Urðarbrunnr—the Well of Fate in Ásgarðr, tended by the three Norns who carve the destinies of gods and men into the bark of the tree itself. The second draws from Mímisbrunnr in Jötunheimr—the Well of Wisdom, for a drink from which Óðinn surrendered one eye without hesitation. The third reaches into Niflheimr and feeds from Hvergelmir, the roaring source of all rivers—beneath which the serpent Níðhöggr gnaws perpetually at the root, working to unravel the foundations of existence.

Yggdrasil is never at rest. A squirrel named Ratatoskr runs its trunk carrying insults between the eagle at the crown and the serpent below, keeping them in perpetual hostility. Four stags roam the branches eating the foliage. The Norns pour water and white clay over the roots each day to keep the tree alive. It is simultaneously being consumed and renewed—a cosmos that tells the truth about itself: nothing is permanent, not even the structure that holds everything together.

This is not a flaw in the Norse cosmological imagination. It is its most honest insight. The appropriate response, in Asatru, is action rather than despair—to live with honor precisely because nothing lasts, in full knowledge of the darkness working at the roots.

The Nine Worlds

The Nine Worlds are not stacked like floors in a building. The Norse sources never give us a precise diagram, and scholars continue to debate their exact arrangement. What the sources make clear is that the worlds are real, distinct, and connected—by Yggdrasil's roots and branches, by rivers that flow between them, by roads that gods, giants, and the occasional adventurous human have traveled.

Ásgarðr — The Realm of the Æsir

Home of the principal Norse gods, Ásgarðr is a realm of great halls and high walls, presided over by Óðinn from his throne Hliðskjálf, from which he can observe all nine realms at once. Within its borders stands Valhöll, where the chosen slain feast and fight while awaiting Ragnarök, and Fólkvangr, the field where Freyja receives her half of those who fall in battle. Ásgarðr is connected to our world by Bifröst, the shimmering rainbow bridge guarded by the ever-watchful Heimdallr.

The gods cross that bridge. They walk among us. Worship in Asatru is the maintenance of a living relationship between beings who, while unequal in power, share a world and a fate—something quite different from the plea of a creature to an untouchable creator.

Vanaheimr — The Realm of the Vanir

Less is known about Vanaheimr than any other world, which is surprising given the importance of the Vanir to modern Heathen practice. The gods of fertility, prosperity, and the cycles of nature—Freyr, Freyja, Njörðr—originated here, yet their homeland is described only in the most general terms: abundant, fertile, ruled by forces older than the Æsir war machine.

The Vanir and Æsir were not always at peace. Their ancient war ended with an exchange of hostages: Freyr, Freyja, and Njörðr came to live among the Æsir, and the two tribes were eventually reconciled into a single tradition. Modern Asatru honors both with equal reverence.

Miðgarðr — The World of Humanity

Miðgarðr means "middle enclosure"—and the name is a theological statement. Humans are not at the center of the cosmos in any position of privilege, but we are at its center in terms of location, surrounded on all sides by forces larger and older than ourselves. The world was fashioned from the body of Ymir, encircled by ocean, and in those waters lies Jörmungandr—the Midgard Serpent, so vast it holds its own tail in its mouth. While it holds, the world holds.

Asatru has no concept of the physical world as something to be transcended or escaped. The earth is the transformed body of the first being; the land spirits that inhabit it are its living presence. To pay attention to rock and river and season, to make offerings to the vættir of a specific place, is to engage with the sacred as the Norse understood it—immediate, local, and inseparable from ordinary life.

Jötunheimr — The Realm of the Giants

Jötunheimr is not simply a land of enemies. The Jötnar—giants—are ancient, often wise, and intimately bound up with the divine order. Óðinn's mother was a giantess. Thor's mother was a giantess. Freyr surrendered his most powerful weapon to win the heart of the giantess Gerðr. The boundaries between gods and giants were never as clean as simple hero-and-monster narratives suggest. Jötunheimr represents the primordial chaos from which order emerged—and to which it will one day return.

Niflheimr and Múspellsheimr — The Primordial Realms

These are the two oldest worlds, the original poles of creation. Niflheimr, world of ice and mist, was the source of the rivers that froze in Ginnungagap. Múspell-sheimr, world of fire and lava, was the heat that melted them. Both realms existed before the gods and will persist after Ragnarök. They are forces of nature in the most absolute sense—present because the cosmos requires both cold and fire, indifferent to the order the gods have built between them.

Álfheimr — The Realm of the Elves

The Ljósálfar—the light elves—inhabit Álfheimr, a realm described as close to Ásgarðr and bathed in brightness. The realm was given to Freyr as a gift at his first tooth. Little else is recorded in the primary sources, but the elves appear throughout the sagas as beings of considerable power, associated with creativity, beauty, and the forces of nature. In modern Asatru, elves are often understood as nature spirits—vættir—closely related to the land itself, deserving of their own offerings and acknowledgment.

Svartálfaheimr — The Realm of the Dwarves

Known also as Niðavellir, this is the underground world of the Dvergar—the dwarves—master craftsmen who produced some of the most powerful objects in all the Nine Worlds: Mjölnir, Thor's hammer; Gungnir, Óðinn's spear; the golden hair of Sif; the binding chain that holds Fenrir. The dwarves represent knowledge applied through skill, the sacred nature of craft. What is made with mastery and intention carries power—a conviction that runs through Asatru's approach to ritual objects and sacred tools to this day.

Helheim — The Realm of the Dead

Helheim is ruled by Hel, daughter of Loki, and it receives the majority of the dead—those who did not fall in battle, who died of age or illness, who lived ordinary lives. It is a place of rest, a shadowed reflection of the living world, presided over by a goddess who, despite her grim reputation, is described in the sources as a keeper rather than a torturer. The Norse afterlife was never primarily organized around reward and damnation. Most people simply continued, in some diminished form, in the realm below Yggdrasil's deepest root. Death, in this understanding, is the completion of a life—not its verdict.

The Norns and the Web of Wyrd

No account of the Norse cosmos is complete without understanding the force that runs through all of it: wyrd—fate, in its Old Norse sense, though the word carries far more weight than its modern equivalent suggests.

The three Norns—Urðr, Verðandi, and Skuld—sit at the base of Yggdrasil beside the Well of Fate, and each day they weave the fates of gods and men into existence, carving them as runes into the bark of the World Tree. Urðr governs what has come to pass, Verðandi what is unfolding now, and Skuld what is yet to become. They are not cruel. They do not punish. They simply weave.

Wyrd was imagined as a vast web in which every action—every choice, every deed, every broken oath and every promise kept—pulls on the threads around it and reshapes what is possible. This is not fatalism. You cannot escape your fate, but you participate in its making. Who you are today was shaped by what others did before you. What you do today shapes the options available to those who come after. This is why ancestors matter in Asatru—not merely as memory, but as active participants in the ongoing fabric of a family's fate.

The web also connects the living to one another. Frið—the peace and loyalty within a community—is not simply a social virtue. It is a cosmological one. Every act of betrayal tears the web. Every act of loyalty strengthens it. The Norns do not judge. But the web remembers everything.

Bifröst: The Bridge Between Worlds

Bifröst is the shimmering rainbow bridge that connects Ásgarðr to Miðgarðr—the passage by which the gods descend into our world and return to their own. Its name is usually interpreted as "the trembling or flickering rainbow," and the sources emphasize its fragility as much as its beauty. It burns at its far end to prevent the frost giants from crossing. It will not survive Ragnarök.

Heimdallr stands eternal watch at its Ásgarðr end, armed with the great horn Gjallarhorn. He sleeps less than a bird, can see for hundreds of miles in any direction, and can hear wool growing on sheep and grass pushing through soil.

When the forces of chaos finally march on Ásgarðr, it will be Heimdallr who sounds the horn that calls the gods to their final battle.

Bifröst matters to practitioners for reasons beyond its narrative role. The bridge is the image of the threshold—the liminal space between the human and the divine. Every ritual space that a Heathen constructs is, in its way, a Bifröst: a deliberate crossing point between the ordinary world and the sacred one. When you step into a ritual circle, light a fire for a blót, or sit in quiet attention before an altar, you are building a bridge—doing what the gods themselves require a rainbow to do.

Ragnarök: The Fate of the Gods

The Norse cosmos does not end with silence. It ends with fire, flood, and the death of gods—and then, improbably, with renewal.

Ragnarök, "the fate of the powers," is the event toward which the entire cosmological structure has always been building. Fenrir breaks his chains. Jörmungandr releases its tail and rises from the ocean. Loki, long imprisoned for his role in Baldr's death, breaks free and leads the forces of chaos toward Ásgarðr. Bifröst shatters under the weight of the fire giants as Surtr leads his armies across it. The gods ride out to meet them knowing, with absolute certainty, that they will not win.

Óðinn is swallowed by Fenrir. Thor kills Jörmungandr and takes nine steps before falling to its venom. Freyr, who gave away his sword for love, falls to Surtr unarmed. Heimdallr and Loki kill each other. Surtr raises his burning blade and sets the world on fire.

Then the earth sinks into the sea. Then it rises again.

Green and renewed, the world re-emerges from the water. A handful of gods survive—among them Baldr, returned from Helheim. A man and woman, Líf and Lífþrasir, who sheltered in Yggdrasil's branches throughout the destruction, emerge to repopulate the world. A new sun—daughter of the old one—rises in the sky.

This cyclical vision of creation and destruction is one of the most distinctive features of the Norse worldview, and one of its most spiritually significant. Other traditions promise that the good will be preserved and evil punished at the end of time. Norse mythology makes no such promise. The gods fight knowing they will fall. They fight anyway—not because victory is guaranteed, but because to stand aside while the world burns is incompatible with honor.

Ragnarök is not a prophecy to fear. It is a model for how to live. You are not promised a good outcome. You are given the choice of how to meet what comes. The Norse gods chose to face their fate with their eyes open and their weapons drawn. In the Heathen tradition, that is the only answer worth giving to the darkness at the roots of the tree.

The Nine Worlds are a map, not a museum exhibit. Asatruar orient themselves by them—every ritual, every offering, every act of worship takes place inside this living framework. In the next chapter, we turn to the texts that preserve this cosmology and ask the question every serious student of Asatru must eventually face: how do we know what we know, and how do we read it wisely?

Chapter 5

The Sacred Texts: Eddas and Sagas

Almost every major religion in the world has a sacred text. A book that serves as the final authority, the fixed point around which all interpretation revolves. Christianity has the Bible. Islam has the Quran. Judaism has the Torah. Followers can disagree about what the text means, but the text itself stands unchanged, authoritative, complete.

Asatru has no such book.

What it has instead is a collection of medieval manuscripts, composed centuries after the conversion of Scandinavia to Christianity, written largely by Christian scholars, in a language spoken natively by very few people alive today. These texts are the primary sources from which modern Heathenry reconstructs its understanding of the gods, the cosmos, and the old ways of worship. They are indispensable, irreplaceable—and deeply imperfect.

Learning to work with them honestly, critically, and with spiritual seriousness is one of the most important skills a practitioner of Asatru can develop. This chapter is a guide to what those texts are, where they came from, and how to read them wisely.

A Living Tradition Put Into Writing

For most of its history, Norse religious knowledge traveled by mouth. Poets memorized thousands of lines of verse and recited them at the courts of kings. Priests—the goðar—passed down ritual knowledge through practice and oral instruction. Stories about the gods were told around fires, at feasts, aboard ships. Writing was not absent from the Norse world—the runic alphabet had existed for centuries—but it was used for inscriptions, not narrative. The idea of sitting down to record the myths of the gods in a book would have struck the ancient Heathens as both unnecessary and slightly absurd. The tradition lived in people, not on pages.

That changed when Christianity arrived.

The conversion of Scandinavia was gradual, spanning roughly from the late ninth to the early twelfth centuries. As the old faith receded, the oral networks that had sustained it began to break down. The skalds who had composed poetry in honor of Odin and Thor still existed, but their audience was shrinking. The myths were still known, but the communities that had kept them alive were fragmenting.

It was in Iceland—the last and most resistant stronghold of the old tradition—that the decision was made to write it down. The scholars who did so were Christian. They wrote in Latin-influenced prose. They approached the old myths with the tools of medieval European historiography, which meant, among other things, that they sometimes rationalized the gods as ancient kings, reframed mythological events as historical ones, and filtered everything through a worldview that regarded the Æsir as false idols rather than living powers.

This is the paradox at the heart of the Asatru textual tradition: the most detailed records of the pre-Christian Norse faith were produced by people who had abandoned it. Every serious practitioner must reckon with this fact. The sources are not a window onto the Viking Age. They are a window onto how educated medieval Icelanders remembered and interpreted the Viking Age, one or two centuries after it ended.

That does not make them worthless. Far from it. But it makes *how* you read them as important as *what* you read.

The Poetic Edda: Voices Without Names

Of all the surviving sources for Norse mythology, the Poetic Edda is the closest to the original oral tradition—raw, fragmentary, and often deliberately obscure in ways that suggest its authors assumed an audience who already knew the stories and needed only the poetic compression, not the explanation.

The collection survives primarily through a single manuscript known as the Codex Regius—the King's Book—which was written down around 1270 CE in Iceland. For nearly four centuries it sat in private hands, largely unknown to the outside world, until 1643, when the Icelandic bishop Brynjólfur Sveinsson acquired it and recognized its significance. He attributed it to the twelfth-century scholar Sæmundr the Learned, which is why the collection is sometimes still called the Sæmundar Edda—though modern scholarship has long since abandoned that attribution. The poems have no single author. They accumulated over generations, shaped and reshaped by the mouths that carried them.

The collection divides broadly into two groups: poems about the gods and poems about heroes. The mythological poems include some of the most important texts in all of Norse literature. The Völuspá—"The Prophecy of the Seeress"—opens with a vision of the cosmos from its creation to Ragnarök, narrated by a völva (a seeress) whom Odin has woken from the dead to question. It is dense, allusive, and deeply strange, written in a voice that addresses Odin directly and seems to take pleasure in the fact that not everything it says can be understood.

The Hávamál—"Sayings of the High One"—is a long didactic poem attributed to Odin himself, containing practical wisdom, gnomic advice, an account of how he won the runes, and a catalog of magical knowledge. Modern Asatruar return to the Hávamál repeatedly; it is the text most often cited as a guide to daily life and personal ethics within the tradition.

The heroic poems deal primarily with figures like Sigurðr the dragon-slayer and the tragic house of the Nibelungs—material that overlaps significantly with the German Nibelungenlied and which fed directly into Wagner's Ring cycle. These poems are less immediately relevant to religious practice, but they illuminate the ethical world the mythology inhabits: a world in which fate is inescapable, loyalty is sacred, and a death met well carries more weight than a life lived safely.

What makes the Poetic Edda invaluable—and difficult—is precisely its resistance to easy interpretation. The poems were composed for audiences already steeped in the mythology, and they make no concessions to the uninitiated. Kennings pile upon kennings; episodes are referenced but not explained; the chronology of mythological events is assumed rather than stated. Reading the Poetic Edda for the first time without a good commentary alongside it is like walking into a conversation already in progress, in a language you mostly but do not entirely speak. The rewards are proportional to the patience you bring.

One question that every reader eventually confronts is the matter of dating. The Codex Regius was written in the thirteenth century, but the poems it contains are generally believed to be older—some possibly predating the conversion, others composed in the century or two immediately following it, when the old stories were still vivid in living memory but Christianity was already reshaping the frame through which they were understood.

Teasing apart what belongs to the pre-Christian tradition and what reflects later Christian influence is one of the central interpretive challenges of Norse scholarship, and it has no clean solution. What practitioners of Asatru can do is read with awareness of this uncertainty—treating the poems as precious but not infallible, inspired but not dictated.

The Prose Edda: Snorri and His Limits

If the Poetic Edda is a fragmentary window onto the old tradition, the Prose Edda is a guided tour—organized, explained, contextualized. It is also, for that very reason, the more dangerous of the two texts to read uncritically.

Snorri Sturluson was an Icelandic chieftain, historian, and poet who lived from 1179 to 1241. He was brilliant, politically ambitious, and thoroughly Christian. He wrote the Prose Edda around 1220 CE with a practical literary aim: to preserve Norse poetic technique—specifically, the complex system of kennings and allusions that skaldic poetry depended upon. To understand why a poet might call the sea "Ymir's blood" or gold "the fire of the Rhine," a reader needed to know the underlying myths. Snorri provided them.

This is crucial to understand, because it means the Prose Edda was written with no religious purpose. Snorri was a scholar rescuing a poetic tradition from obsolescence, not a theologian of the old faith. In doing so, he organized and rationalized material that had originally been far more fluid, resolving contradictions, smoothing over ambiguities, and occasionally imposing a coherence onto the mythology that it may not originally have had.

He also approached the gods through a distinctly medieval Christian lens known as euhemerism—the theory, popular in medieval Europe, that pagan gods were originally human kings and warriors whose deeds had been mythologized over time. In the prologue to the Prose Edda, Snorri presents the Æsir as a tribe of great men from Asia who traveled to Scandinavia and were eventually worshipped as gods by the people they conquered. This was an attempt to make the tradition intellectually respectable within a Christian worldview, not to honor it on its own terms.

None of this makes the Prose Edda unusable. It remains the single most complete account of Norse cosmology and mythology that survives, and without it, our knowledge of the Nine Worlds, the creation myth, and the narrative of Ragnarök would be drastically thinner. But it should never be read in isolation, and its author's perspective should always be kept in mind. Where Snorri and the Poetic Edda agree, confidence is warranted. Where only Snorri says something, caution is appropriate. Where he explains the inner meaning of a myth with suspicious tidiness, skepticism is healthy.

The Sagas: Belief in the Texture of Daily Life

The Eddas tell us what the Norse believed about the cosmos and the gods. The sagas show us how those beliefs played out in the daily fabric of human life—a distinction that matters enormously to anyone approaching these texts as a practitioner rather than a scholar.

The Icelandic sagas are prose narratives composed between the twelfth and fourteenth centuries, dealing primarily with the lives of Icelandic families during the settlement period of the ninth and tenth centuries. They are not mythological texts and do not describe the gods in any systematic way. What they do—sometimes in passing, sometimes at length—is reveal the texture of a world in which the old beliefs were still living: a world where a man might make an offering to the land spirits before plowing a new field, where a woman's prophetic dreams carried legal weight at the Thing, where the dead could walk if they were not properly buried, and where the relationship between the living and their ancestors was understood as ongoing rather than closed by death.

Several categories of saga material deserve particular attention. The Íslendingasögur—the sagas of the Icelanders—are the most historically grounded and contain scattered but valuable details about how ordinary people practiced their faith. The fornaldarsögur—the legendary sagas—are more overtly mythological, dealing with heroes, giants, and sorcery, and they overlap in interesting ways with the heroic material in the Poetic Edda. The konungasögur—the kings' sagas—include Snorri's own Heimskringla, which opens with the Ynglinga saga, a semi-mythological history of the earliest Norse kings that contains some of the most detailed descriptions of pre-Christian ritual practice found anywhere in the literature.

A concrete example helps. The Eyrbyggja saga—one of the Íslendingasögur—describes in passing how a local chieftain maintains a private temple, conducts seasonal blóts, and mediates between his community and the land spirits of the Snæfellsnes peninsula. None of this is the point of the story; the narrative is concerned with feuds, legal disputes, and the particular stubbornness of several generations of difficult men. But precisely because the religious details are incidental rather than expository, they carry a different kind of authority than a systematic account would. The author is not explaining paganism to an audience that doesn't know it. He is simply describing how people lived. The Heimskringla offers something different in register but equally valuable: Snorri's account of King Hákon the Good, a Christian king forced to participate in the blót at Lade against his will, gives one of the most vivid surviving descriptions of a large communal sacrifice—the preparation of the hall, the blessing of the drinking horns, the toasts to Odin and the other gods—precisely because Snorri is documenting something that, by his era, had already passed.

What this means practically is that the sagas reward a particular kind of reading attention: noticing the religious detail that appears without fanfare, the offering made before a journey, the dream taken seriously as prophecy, the dead man whose grave mound the family continues to visit. These moments are not always historically reliable—but their very casualness is often the strongest argument that they reflect something real about how the tradition was actually lived.

Reading the sagas with the same critical awareness demanded by the Eddas requires an additional complication: the sagas blend history, fiction, and folklore in proportions that vary from text to text and sometimes from chapter to chapter. A blót described in one saga may reflect actual pre-Christian practice. It may also reflect a Christian author's assumptions about what pagans did. Distinguishing between the two requires context, comparison, and a willingness to hold uncertainty without anxiety—a quality that, as we will see in the next section, Asatru regards as a spiritual virtue in itself.

How to Read These Texts as an Asatruar

No serious practitioner of Asatru treats the Eddas or the sagas the way a fundamentalist treats scripture—as literal, inerrant, and final. The sources are too inconsistent for that, too shaped by the hands that recorded them, too full of gaps that honest scholarship cannot fill.

What modern Heathenry has developed instead is a working distinction between lore and UPG—Unverified Personal Gnosis. Lore is what the texts actually say. UPG is the personal spiritual understanding that a practitioner develops through ritual, meditation, and direct experience of the divine—insights that feel true and meaningful but cannot be sourced to any surviving manuscript. Both have a legitimate place in Asatru. The lore provides the shared framework that makes community worship possible. UPG provides the living, personal dimension without which any faith calcifies into performance.

The practical stakes of this distinction become clear the moment you try to reconstruct something the sources don't cover. Take the question of how a solitary practitioner should conduct a blót without a kindred, a goði, or a purpose-built altar. The primary sources assume a communal context; they describe large gatherings, shared drinking horns, priests officiating before assembled households. They say almost nothing about individual practice, because individual practice in that world was embedded in community life in ways that made it invisible as a separate category. The lore, here, simply goes silent.

A practitioner facing that silence has a few options. They can extrapolate from what the texts do say—if the blót's essential structure is hallowing, sharing, and libation, those elements can be maintained at a smaller scale with a single cup and a patch of earth. They can draw on comparative material from related traditions. Or they can work from their own experience of what feels coherent and alive within the framework the lore has established. All three approaches produce UPG of varying degrees of distance from the textual record—and being clear about that distance is itself an act of intellectual honesty that the tradition's emphasis on truth demands.

This is why serious Heathens tend to specify, in discussion, whether something they're describing is lore or UPG. Not gatekeeping—rather, a way of keeping the shared framework stable while preserving space for the personal and the experiential. The tradition holds both, and knowing which is which makes both more useful.

The tension between the two is not a problem to be solved. It is the engine of a living tradition. Practitioners disagree—sometimes vigorously—about how closely modern practice should follow the textual record, how much weight to give Snorri's interpretations, and how freely the gaps in the sources can be filled by intuition and innovation. These disagreements are healthy. A religion that demands uniform interpretation of imperfect texts is not a religion built on honor and independent judgment. Asatru has always been both.

Start with the Hávamál and the Völuspá. Read them slowly, with a good commentary alongside. Follow the threads that interest you into the sagas. Return to the texts repeatedly as your practice deepens—you will find different things in them each time. The goal is not mastery of the material. The goal is a living relationship with a tradition that has survived, imperfectly and magnificently, across more than a thousand years.

The texts preserve the stories. The next chapter introduces the beings at the center of them—the gods and goddesses of the Norse pantheon, and the distinct relationship that Asatru builds with each of them.

Chapter 6

Norse Mythology

N orse mythology is not a theology. It contains no commandments, no promises of salvation, no systematic account of what you must believe to be counted among the faithful. What it contains instead is something older and, in many ways, more honest: stories. Stories about gods who make mistakes and giants who possess wisdom, about wars that end in uneasy peace, about treasures forged in darkness and deaths that reshape the universe. These stories were never meant to be read as literal history or accepted as divine revelation. They were meant to be lived with—turned over in the mind, argued about, returned to across a lifetime of practice.

The myths serve a specific spiritual function in Asatru. They are not doctrine. They are a mirror—a way of understanding the forces that shape the cosmos and, by extension, the forces that shape a human life. When Odin sacrifices his eye for wisdom, he is not simply a character in an ancient story. He is a model for what it means to pursue knowledge seriously, to understand that insight always costs something. When Thor crosses into Jötunheimr unarmed and outwitted, he is not simply being humiliated. He is demonstrating that even the strongest among us are vulnerable when stripped of our tools and our certainties.

This chapter surveys the major stories, beings, and mythological cycles that form the living core of the Asatru tradition. Some of the figures you will meet here—the Æsir gods—will be explored in greater depth in the following chapter. What matters here is not the catalog but the pattern: the way these stories fit together into a coherent vision of a world built on conflict, sustained by relationships, and moving toward an end that is also a renewal.

The War of Gods: Æsir and Vanir

The Norse mythological tradition does not begin in harmony. Before the world as we know it was fully settled, before the walls of Ásgarðr were complete, two families of gods went to war with each other—and the consequences of that war echo through every myth that follows.

The Æsir, led by Óðinn, were gods of sovereignty, war, and social order. Their world was structured, hierarchical, governed by oaths and contracts. The Vanir—Freyr, Freya, Njörðr—were gods of fertility, magic, and the rhythms of the natural world. Where the Æsir built walls, the Vanir moved with the seasons. Where the Æsir valued honor earned through conflict, the Vanir understood power as something that grew, like grain, in its own time.

What exactly sparked the war is unclear even in the primary sources. The Völuspá hints that it began when a Vanir woman named Gullveig arrived in Ásgarðr and was killed—three times—by the Æsir, who burned her body and could not keep her dead. She rose each time, and the Vanir took the attack as a declaration of war. The fighting that followed was long and inconclusive. Neither side could decisively defeat the other. Eventually, exhausted and roughly matched, they chose peace.

The peace was sealed in the old way: an exchange of hostages. Njörðr, Freyr, and Freya went to live among the Æsir. In return, the Æsir sent Hœnir and the wise Mímir to Vanaheimr. The arrangement did not go smoothly on the Vanir side. Hœnir proved to be a poor counselor without Mímir's guidance—impressive in bearing but empty without his advisor beside him. The Vanir, feeling deceived, killed Hœnir and cut off Mímir's head, sending it back to Ásgarðr. Óðinn, rather than returning to war, preserved the head with herbs and runes and kept Mímir as an oracle—still consulting him at the roots of Yggdrasil for wisdom that only the dead can offer.

The peace held. The Vanir gods settled into Ásgarðr and became, in time, indistinguishable members of the divine community. Freya taught Óðinn the art of seiðr—a form of magic associated with fate-manipulation and shape-shifting, previously the province of the Vanir. That Óðinn, king of the Æsir, learned his most powerful magic from a Vanir woman is one of the mythology's most telling details. The gods grow by what they absorb from those they once fought.

From the mingled spittle of the two divine clans—an ancient ritual of peace-making—the gods created Kvasir, the wisest being who ever lived. He wandered the Nine Worlds answering every question put to him, satisfying every inquiry, until two dwarves named Fjalarr and Galarr murdered him and drained his blood into three vessels. Mixed with honey, that blood became the Mead of Poetry—the draught that confers the gift of eloquence and poetic inspiration on whoever drinks it. Óðinn eventually obtained the mead through a combination of seduction, deception, and outright theft, and brought it back to Ásgarðr, where it became the source of all great poetry in the human world. When a skald composed a verse of unusual power, the Norse understood it as a drop of Kvasir's blood finding its way home.

The Æsir-Vanir War is, at its core, a myth about integration—two ways of understanding the sacred that initially appear incompatible and eventually discover they need each other. The ordered, contractual world of the Æsir without the fertility and magic of the Vanir would be sterile. The natural abundance of the Vanir without the structure of the Æsir would be ungoverned. The tradition that emerged from their war and their peace is richer than either would have been alone.

The Jötnar: The Chaos the World Requires

No figure in Norse mythology is more consistently misunderstood than the giant. Popular culture has reduced the Jötnar to monsters—obstacles for the gods to defeat, crude forces of destruction with no interior life and no claim on our sympathy. The actual mythological tradition is far more complicated, and understanding its complexity is essential to understanding how the Norse cosmos actually works.

The word Jötunn (plural Jötnar) does not mean "giant" in the sense of a very large human. Its root in Proto-Germanic suggests something closer to "devourer"—a being that consumes, overwhelms, breaks down. The Jötnar are forces of dissolution, of entropy, of the wild and unordered aspects of reality. They are not evil in any moral sense. They are simply what reality looks like when it has not yet been shaped by divine will—or when that shaping has started to come undone.

The Jötnar were among the first beings in existence. Ymir, the primordial giant from whose body the gods built the world, was the ancestor of all of them. The frost giants who inhabit Jötunheimr are his descendants. The fire giants of Muspelheim, led by Surtr, represent the other primordial pole—heat and destruction rather than cold and stasis. Between these two extremes, the cosmos was created, and between these two extremes, it will eventually end.

What makes the Jötnar so interesting—and so theologically important—is how blurred the boundary between them and the gods actually is. Óðinn's mother was a giantess. Thor's mother, Jörð, was a giantess—the earth itself personified. Freyr gave up his sword for the love of the giantess Gerðr, a sacrifice so costly it will contribute directly to his death at Ragnarök. The gods travel to Jötunheimr constantly—to seek wisdom, to find lovers, to recover stolen property. Many of the Jötnar are beautiful, intelligent, and complex. Skadi, the mountain giantess who came to Ásgarðr seeking revenge for her father's death, was persuasive enough to negotiate her own terms with the gods and ended up marrying among the Æsir. She is now honored as a goddess in her own right by many modern Asatruar.

Among the most important Jötnar is Loki—a figure who resists every simple categorization the mythology offers. He is listed as a frost giant by ancestry, son of Fárbauti and Laufey, but he lives in Ásgarðr as Óðinn's sworn blood brother. He is the father—or, in one case, the mother—of some of the most dangerous beings in the cosmos: Fenrir, the wolf fated to swallow Óðinn at Ragnarök; Jörmungandr, the Midgard Serpent; and Hel, ruler of the realm of the dead. He is also the mother, through shapeshifting, of Sleipnir, Óðinn's eight-legged horse. Loki is the mythology's great disruptor—the force that makes things happen, that introduces chaos into divine order and occasionally produces something invaluable in the process. Without Loki, Thor would never have gotten Mjölnir. Without Loki, Ásgarðr's walls might never have been built. Without Loki, Baldr would still be alive—and the cosmos would have no reason to move toward Ragnarök.

Fenrir deserves particular attention. Raised by the gods themselves in an attempt to control him, he grew at a rate that alarmed even the Æsir, and they eventually bound him with a magical chain forged by the dwarves—so light it appeared to be made of silk, yet unbreakable. Fenrir agreed to be bound only if one of the gods would place a hand in his mouth as a guarantee of good faith. Only Tyr accepted. When Fenrir found he could not break free, he bit off Tyr's hand. The god of justice lost his sword hand to keep the wolf contained—a sacrifice accepted with characteristic Norse stoicism, as the price of maintaining order in the cosmos for as long as possible.

Hrungnir, the stone-hearted giant, challenged Óðinn to a horse race and ended up as Thor's most famous opponent in single combat. Thrym, king of the frost giants, stole Mjölnir and demanded Freya as ransom—a scheme that ended with Thor disguised as a bride, Loki as his handmaiden, and an entire hall of giants destroyed. Angrboda, Loki's giantess partner and mother of his three monstrous children, embodies the principle that the most dangerous forces in the cosmos are also the most generative. Her children will end the world. But the world, the mythology insists, needs ending—so that something better can begin.

The Jötnar are not enemies to be denounced but forces to be understood. They represent the aspects of reality that resist domestication: winter, death, the sea in storm, the hunger that no harvest fully satisfies. A faith that pretended these forces did not exist would be dishonest about the world it inhabits. Asatru has always been willing to look at the darkness and name it clearly.

Three Mythological Cycles

The Norse myths do not arrange themselves into a single linear narrative. They cluster instead around recurring themes—loss, theft, betrayal, sacrifice—and the same characters reappear in different configurations, testing the same values under different pressures. Three cycles in particular stand at the center of the tradition, and every serious student of Asatru will return to them repeatedly.

The Death of Baldr

Of all the myths in the Norse tradition, the death of Baldr is the one that resonates most deeply across cultures—because it is, at its core, a story about the thing that cannot be prevented, no matter how much love is brought to bear against it.

Baldr, son of Óðinn and Frigg, was the most beloved of all the gods. Wise, radiant, and graceful, he was the one figure in the Norse pantheon about whom no one—god, giant, dwarf, or elf—had a single hostile word. When he began to suffer prophetic dreams of his own death, Frigg moved through all the Nine Worlds and extracted a promise from every living thing—stone and metal, fire and water, animal and plant—that none of them would harm her son. The gods celebrated by making sport of Baldr's new invulnerability, hurling weapons at him that bounced harmlessly away.

Frigg had overlooked one thing: mistletoe. Too young, too small, too seemingly insignificant to bother with—or so she reasoned. Loki found this out through deception, shaped a dart from the plant, and placed it in the hands of Baldr's blind brother Höðr, guiding his throw. Baldr fell dead.

The grief of the gods was total. Óðinn placed his golden ring Draupnir on the funeral pyre. Thor consecrated the ship with Mjölnir. The giantess Hyrrokkin, summoned to launch the funeral vessel because no Æsir was strong enough to move it alone, pushed it into the sea with a single shove that sent sparks flying from the rollers. Frigg sent her son Hermóðr to Helheim to negotiate Baldr's return. Hel agreed to release him on one condition: every being in the Nine Worlds must weep for him. And every being did—except one. A giantess named Þökk, almost certainly Loki in disguise, refused. Baldr remained in Helheim. He will return only after Ragnarök, in the world reborn from the ashes of the old.

The myth carries several layers of meaning worth sitting with. The most obvious is the simplest: even the most beloved, most protected thing in the cosmos can be lost. No amount of love, preparation, or precaution constitutes a guarantee. Frigg's grief is real and her effort was total—and it was not enough. The Norse worldview does not offer comfort of the false kind.

But there is a second layer. Baldr's death is not only a tragedy. It is a necessary event in the movement of the cosmos toward Ragnarök and, beyond it, renewal. The world that exists after Ragnarök—green, reborn, populated by the survivors among both gods and humans—is a better world, and Baldr walks in it. His death, and the impossibility of preventing it, are part of a pattern larger than any single grief. This does not make the grief smaller. It makes the pattern worth trusting.

The Binding of Fenrir

The binding of Fenrir is a myth about the price of security, and it does not allow the reader to feel entirely comfortable about that price.

Fenrir grew in Ásgarðr at a rate that alarmed the gods. They attempted to bind him twice with chains of their own forging, and twice he snapped them effortlessly, apparently enjoying the game. For the third attempt, they commissioned the dwarves of Svartálfaheimr to create something that could not be broken—not through strength but through craft. The result was Gleipnir: a ribbon of impossible lightness, made from the sound of a cat's footstep, the beard of a woman, the roots of a mountain, the sinews of a bear, the breath of a fish, and the spittle of a bird. Things that do not exist, bound together into something that cannot be undone.

Fenrir was suspicious of anything so light and delicate. He would only allow himself to be bound if one of the gods placed a hand in his mouth as a pledge that the chain would be removed if he could not break free. None of the gods were willing. None except Tyr, who placed his sword hand between the wolf's jaws without hesitation.

When Fenrir found he could not break free, he bit off Tyr's hand at the wrist. The god of justice—of the sacred oath, of the fair terms of engagement—paid with his sword hand for the binding that would hold until Ragnarök. He accepted this not with rage but with the recognition that some costs are simply the cost of maintaining the order that makes civilization possible.

The figure of Tyr standing with his hand in the wolf's mouth is one of the most powerful images the tradition offers. It is a picture of what it means to act justly when justice is expensive—to hold to the terms of an agreement even when the agreement costs you everything you use to enforce agreements. Tyr lost his hand. He did not lose his honor. In the Asatru moral framework, that is the only distinction that finally matters.

The Theft of Thor's Hammer

If the death of Baldr and the binding of Fenrir are myths of tragic necessity, the theft of Mjölnir is something entirely different: a myth of cunning, comedy, and the kind of problem-solving that requires a god of thunder to dress as a bride.

Thrym, king of the frost giants, stole Mjölnir while Thor slept and buried it eight leagues beneath the earth. His ransom demand was Freya, the most beautiful of all the goddesses, as his wife. Freya's response to this proposal was so furious that the walls of Ásgarðr shook. The gods convened in emergency council. It was Heimdallr—the far-sighted, the one who misses nothing—who proposed the solution: Thor himself would go to Jötunheimr disguised as the bride, with Loki as his handmaiden.

Thor's objections to this plan were extensive. Loki's counter-arguments were efficient. Thor put on the dress.

What followed in Thrym's hall is one of the funniest passages in the entire mythological corpus. Thor ate an ox, eight salmon, and all the delicacies prepared for the women, and drank three barrels of mead. Thrym, slightly alarmed, observed that he had never seen a bride with such an appetite. Loki explained that the lady had been so eager for this marriage that she had not eaten in eight days. Thrym leaned forward to steal a kiss beneath the veil and recoiled from the burning intensity of Thor's eyes. Loki explained that the lady had not slept in eight days either, so great was her longing. When Thrym ordered Mjölnir brought forth to consecrate the wedding—as was the custom, the hammer being used to bless marriages as well as to break skulls—Thor had what he needed. He seized it, killed Thrym, and killed every giant in the hall before leaving.

The myth is comic in tone but serious in implication. Mjölnir was not simply Thor's personal weapon. It was the instrument by which the gods maintained the boundary between order and chaos, the tool that consecrated births, weddings, and deaths, the symbol of the protective force that kept Miðgarðr from being overrun. Its theft was an existential crisis disguised as a domestic problem. The solution required a willingness to set aside dignity completely in service of the actual goal—a lesson that has not lost its relevance.

The Dwarves: Craftsmen of the Cosmos

The Dvergar—the dwarves—occupy a peculiar position in the Norse mythological hierarchy. They are not gods. They are not giants. They are not the cheerful underground miners of later European folklore. They are something older and stranger: beings who emerged, according to the Prose Edda, from the body of Ymir himself, forming in his flesh like maggots in dead meat before the gods gave them consciousness and the shapes of men. Their origins are rooted in death, and their world—Svartálfaheimr, also called Niðavellir—is deep underground, lit only by the fires of their forges.

What the dwarves possess, in compensation for their chthonic origins, is an unmatched mastery of craft. Everything of real power in the Norse cosmos was made by dwarf hands. Mjölnir, capable of leveling mountains, came from the forge of Brokkr and Eitri. Gungnir, Óðinn's spear, which never misses its mark, was made by the sons of Ívaldi. Gleipnir, the unbreakable ribbon that holds Fenrir, was dwarf-work. Draupnir, the gold ring that replicates itself every nine nights, producing eight rings of equal weight, was made in the same commission as Mjölnir, as part of a wager Loki made with his own head on the line—a wager he narrowly won by insisting, with characteristic technicality, that the dwarves had rights to his head but not his neck.

The gods obtained these treasures through various combinations of negotiation, trickery, and outright manipulation, and the stories of their acquisition are among the most entertaining in the entire tradition. When Loki cut off Sif's golden hair as a prank and Thor threatened to break every bone in his body, Loki went underground and commissioned not only replacement hair for Sif but two additional gifts to placate the other gods—Skiðblaðnir, the ship that can sail any sea and be folded into a pocket, and Gungnir. Then, recklessly, he bet his head against the ability of two other dwarves to produce something better, and they created Gullinbursti, Draupnir, and Mjölnir. When the gods judged Mjölnir the greatest treasure in the Nine Worlds, Loki was technically obliged to forfeit his head—and escaped by insisting on the neck clause. The dwarves settled for sewing his mouth shut instead, which the tradition suggests was, all things considered, a reasonable outcome.

Beyond their role as providers of divine equipment, the dwarves represent a principle that runs deep in Asatru: that craft is a form of sacred knowledge. What is made with real skill, with full attention and the right intention, carries power that raw materials alone cannot provide. The dwarves work in darkness, by firelight, with complete absorption—and what emerges from their forges shapes the fate of gods. Practitioners who work in traditional crafts—woodworking, weaving, smithing, carving—often understand their work through this lens. The act of making something well is an act of participating in the same creative force that produced Mjölnir.

Elves and the Spirits of the Land

The line between gods, elves, and land spirits in Norse mythology is not a line at all. It is a gradient—a slow shift from one category to another, with no clear boundary and no authoritative map. This ambiguity is not a failure of the tradition's systematizing impulse. It reflects something true about how the pre-Christian Norse experienced the sacred: as something present everywhere, in varying intensities, rather than confined to specific beings in specific places.

The Ljósálfar—the light elves—are described in the Prose Edda as more beautiful than the sun, dwelling in Álfheimr under the stewardship of Freyr. Beyond this, the primary sources say remarkably little about them in systematic terms. What they do say, scattered across the Eddas and sagas, suggests beings of considerable power—associated with creativity, beauty, health, and the vital forces of the natural world. The distinction between elves and the Vanir gods is unclear even within the tradition itself. One Old Norse poem refers to the Vanir simply as elves. Freyr rules their realm. The boundaries, it seems, were understood to be permeable.

The Svartálfar—the dark elves—are even more ambiguous. In many sources they appear to be simply another name for the dwarves, connected to death and the underground rather than to light and the upper world. Whether they represent a distinct category of being or a different way of naming the same beings in a different context is a question the primary sources do not resolve, and modern scholarship has not settled.

More immediately relevant to Asatru practice are the landvættir—the land spirits. These are beings who inhabit specific features of the physical landscape: a particular tree, a waterfall, a stretch of coastline, a mountain pass. They are presences, with personalities, preferences, and the capacity for both blessing and harm. The early Icelandic law codes—among the most practical documents to survive from the Norse world—required ships approaching Iceland to remove the dragon-heads from their prows so as not to frighten the land spirits of the coast. This was not poetic metaphor. It was legal requirement, reflecting a lived understanding that the land was inhabited by beings whose goodwill mattered.

The spirits could ensure the fertility of the fields, the health of the livestock, the safety of those who traveled through their territory. In return, they expected acknowledgment—through small offerings, through respectful behavior on their land, through the simple act of awareness that they were present. A farmer who ignored the landvættir of his fields was not being irreligious in any formal sense. He was being rude to his neighbors, with predictable consequences.

The connection between land spirits and human ancestors adds another layer of complexity. In the Old Norse tradition, the dead did not always travel far. Many remained associated with the land they had worked during their lives, inhabiting burial mounds, continuing to influence the fertility of the soil above them, occasionally appearing to the living in dreams or visions. The boundary between a revered ancestor and a local land spirit could be so thin as to be functionally nonexistent. King Óláfr Geirstaðaálfr—literally "Ólaf the Elf of Geirstaðr"—was a Norwegian king whose burial mound became a site of offerings, and whose name suggests that he was understood to have become, in death, the presiding spirit of his territory.

This fluidity has direct implications for Asatru practice today. Many contemporary Heathens maintain a relationship with the landvættir of their specific location—acknowledging them when moving to a new place, making small offerings at significant points in the seasonal calendar, and approaching the natural features of their environment with deliberate attention rather than casual indifference. This is not nature worship in any vague, undifferentiated sense. It is the recognition that the place where you live is inhabited, that its inhabitants have been there longer than you have, and that a good neighbor introduces himself.

The worship of elves—like the worship of ancestors—survived the formal conversion of the Norse peoples to Christianity by centuries. Medieval law codes continued to prohibit elf-offerings long after they had stopped bothering to prohibit the worship of Óðinn and Thor. Whatever the elves were, they were close enough to daily life that people were not prepared to let them go.

Valkyries and the Einherjar

The modern image of the Valkyrie—noble, beautiful, carrying fallen warriors to Valhalla on white horses—is not wrong. It is simply incomplete, and the part that has been left out changes the picture considerably.

The name Valkyrja means "chooser of the slain." In its earlier, pre-literary form, the emphasis was on the second half of that phrase as much as the first. The Valkyries did not only choose which of the dead would be honored with a place in Valhalla. They chose who would die. They moved through the battlefield before the fighting was over, selecting their favorites among the living and ensuring, through a combination of direct influence and the weaving of fate, that those selections would be realized. In the poem Darraðarljóð, preserved in Njal's Saga, twelve Valkyries sit at a loom before the Battle of Clontarf, weaving the fate of the warriors with a warp of human entrails, weights of severed heads, and beaters of swords and arrows. They weave, and men die in the pattern they have chosen. This is not a comforting image. It was not meant to be.

In later traditions, as the mythology was filtered through more literary and romantic sensibilities, the Valkyries became primarily figures of service and love—the beautiful attendants of Valhalla, the swan maidens who occasionally took mortal husbands and were bound to them by the possession of their feather cloaks. Both aspects were always present in the tradition. The earlier, darker version simply received less attention as the Viking Age receded and the stories passed through increasingly Christian hands.

Understanding the Valkyries as Óðinn's projections helps make sense of both their power and their apparent paradox. They are extensions of the Allfather—like his ravens Huginn and Muninn, semi-independent aspects of a larger will, sent out into the world to gather what he needs. What Óðinn needs, always, is warriors. Not because he values battle for its own sake, but because he is preparing for Ragnarök with the clarity of a general who knows the odds and intends to fight anyway. Every warrior the Valkyries bring to Valhalla is another soldier in the army that will stand with him at the end of the world. The feast, the mead, the daily combat that heals by nightfall—all of it is preparation.

The Einherjar—the chosen dead who inhabit Valhalla—are the other half of this picture. Their name translates roughly as "those who fight alone" or, in an older interpretation, "those who belong to an army." They are the elite warriors who died in battle and were deemed worthy of Óðinn's hall, where they spend eternity in a cycle of combat and feasting that would have struck any living Viking as an extraordinarily appealing afterlife. They fight each morning and their wounds close by evening. They eat the boar Sæhrímnir, who is slaughtered and resurrected daily. They drink mead from the goat Heiðrún, whose udder never runs dry. The Valkyries serve them and tend them. They lack for nothing except, perhaps, the final battle they are being prepared for.

It is easy to read Valhalla as simple wish fulfillment—a warrior culture's fantasy of the perfect afterlife. But the deeper structure of the myth resists that reading. The Einherjar are not in Valhalla because they were rewarded. They are there because they were chosen for a purpose. Óðinn is not running a paradise. He is running a training ground for an army he knows will lose. The warriors he selects are the best he can gather, and they will fight with everything they have at Ragnarök, and they will fall with the gods. The feast is real. The mead is real. And the knowledge that all of it ends in a battle that cannot be won is also real, and is never hidden from them.

The Valkyries and Einherjar are figures of total commitment—to a cause, to a community, to a willingness to stand and fight in full knowledge of the outcome. The Einherjar did not choose their fate. They chose how to meet it. That distinction is the one the Asatru tradition has always considered most worth honoring.

Ancestors, Draugr, and the Living Dead

The Norse relationship with the dead was not one of clean separation. Death did not remove a person from the community. It changed their role within it.

Ancestor veneration was among the most widespread and persistent practices in pre-Christian Norse culture, and it required no elaborate theology to justify. The dead were present. They remained connected to the land they had worked, the family they had raised, the reputation they had built. Their hamingja—the luck understood as a semi-independent aspect of the self, capable of being passed down through bloodlines—continued to operate in the world after their physical death, shaping the fortunes of their descendants in ways that could be cultivated or neglected. To honor your ancestors was not sentiment. It was practical acknowledgment of a living relationship with forces that continued to affect your life.

The most visible form this took was the burial mound. Graves were placed on the edges of farmsteads and fields, where the dead could watch over the land they had once tended. Their continued presence was understood as a source of fertility—the biological logic of decomposition given sacred meaning. Descendants seeking creative inspiration or answers to pressing questions would sit atop the grave mound of a revered ancestor, a practice called útiseta (sitting out), and wait for what came. The ancestors were consulted. They responded. The relationship was ongoing, maintained by offerings, by remembrance, by speaking the names of the dead aloud at seasonal gatherings.

Offerings to the ancestors formed part of the dísablót—a seasonal ritual honoring the dísir, female ancestral spirits who watched over families and could intervene in both birth and death. The dísir were the accumulated feminine power of a family line, sometimes fierce, sometimes nurturing, always present. To neglect them was to cut yourself off from a source of protection that no living person could fully replace.

The draugr represents the dark inversion of the honored ancestor—what a dead person becomes when the relationship between the living and the dead breaks down catastrophically. Where the respected ancestor brings fertility and protection, the draugr brings destruction, disease, and death. It rises from the grave not in peace but in rage, driven by the unresolved energies of a life that ended badly—through violence, dishonor, improper burial, or an obsessive attachment to possessions or grievances that the dead person could not release.

The draugr of the sagas are not subtle. They grow to enormous size, possess superhuman strength, smell of decay, and appear to take real pleasure in the suffering they cause. The Eyrbyggja saga describes a draugr so massive and heavy that it could not be moved without levers. Unlike the mindless zombies of modern entertainment, the Norse draugr retained human intelligence—which made them considerably more dangerous, capable of strategy and of a particular kind of sadism that purely animal aggression cannot produce. They preyed on livestock as well as humans, strangling animals in the fields and driving entire communities from their land.

The remedies were correspondingly extreme. The most reliable method was exhumation—digging up the corpse, severing the head, and burning the remains before scattering the ashes at sea. A hero willing to wrestle the draugr back into its grave and remove its head in hand-to-hand combat was another option, though not an appealing one. Preventive measures included binding the toes of the corpse together, driving needles through the feet, and placing heavy stones on the grave to prevent the dead from rising in the first place.

The draugr is a mythological statement about what happens when the relationship between the living and the dead is severed or dishonored—when the dead are not properly mourned, not properly remembered, not properly sent on their way. The practice of ancestor veneration, of speaking the names of the dead and making offerings at the seasonal festivals, is in part a way of ensuring that no one in your family line has reason to return in anger. You care for your dead so that they, in turn, can care for you.

Other Beings

The Norse cosmos is populated beyond the capacity of any single chapter to exhaust. Several figures deserve at least a brief introduction.

Sol and Mani—sun and moon—ride horse-drawn chariots across the sky, pursued without rest by the wolves Hati and Sköll. Their eternal chase will end at Ragnarök when the wolves finally catch them, plunging the world into darkness before the new sun—Sol's daughter—rises over the reborn world. They are among the oldest figures in the entire Germanic tradition, their images found on Bronze Age rock carvings centuries before the Viking Age, suggesting a continuity of worship that outlasted every other shift in religious sensibility.

Trolls in the Norse tradition bear little resemblance to their later fairy-tale descendants. They are large, dangerous, and associated with the wild places where human order breaks down—deep forests, high mountains, the margins of the settled world. Some can be repelled by steel or sunlight; some turn to stone at dawn. They represent, at the level of folk belief, the same principle the Jötnar represent at the cosmic level: the persistence of the untamed, the limits of human control over a landscape that was never fully domesticated and never will be.

The Norns, already discussed in Chapter 4, deserve mention here in their mythological context. They appear in individual destinies as well as cosmic ones—present at the birth of every child, weaving the threads of that specific life into the larger fabric. A person's fate was not their punishment or their reward. It was the unique configuration of possibilities that the Norns had shaped from the raw material of who they were and who their ancestors had been. Working with that fate rather than against it—understanding it clearly enough to act within it with intelligence and honor—is one of the central practical concerns of Asatru to this day.

The beings and stories in this chapter are a living presence in the Asatru tradition—the inherited wisdom of a people who understood the cosmos as animated, relational, and demanding of active engagement. Every figure we have met, from Kvasir to the draugr, from the Valkyries to the landvættir, maps a different aspect of a single consistent vision: a world that rewards attention, punishes neglect, and offers no guarantees except the enduring value of how you choose to meet whatever comes.

In the next chapter, we turn from the mythological landscape to its central inhabitants—the gods and goddesses of the Norse pantheon—and explore the specific relationships that Asatruar build with each of them.

Chapter 7

Meeting the Gods

K nowing a god's story and having a relationship with that god are two different things. The previous chapter told you who the Norse gods are—their myths, their roles in the cosmic order, the stories that have preserved them across a thousand years. This chapter asks a different question: how do you actually meet them?

In Asatru, the gods are not historical figures to be studied or moral authorities to be obeyed. They are living presences—forces within the cosmos that can be approached, honored, petitioned, and, over time, known. The relationship a practitioner builds with the divine is personal, reciprocal, and cumulative. It deepens through ritual, through offerings, through the discipline of returning to the same practice again and again until something begins to respond.

Many Asatruar develop a particular connection with one deity above all others—a fulltrúi, meaning "fully trusted one," a divine patron with whom they feel a specific affinity. This is not a formal initiation or a permanent binding. It grows organically, through practice and attention, and it does not preclude honoring other gods. Think of it less like choosing a religion and more like recognizing a friendship that was already forming.

What follows is a practical introduction to the major figures of the Norse pantheon—not their stories, but their character, their domains, and the ways in which modern Asatruar bring them into daily life.

The Major Gods

Óðinn

Domain: Wisdom, poetry, magic, war, death, sovereignty.

Of all the Norse gods, Óðinn is the most demanding and the least predictable. He is the Allfather—the oldest, the most powerful, the most willing to pay impossible prices for knowledge. He gave his eye. He hanged on Yggdrasil for nine days. He consults the severed head of Mímir. He sends his ravens into the world each day and waits for what they bring back.

Practitioners drawn to Óðinn tend to be those for whom the pursuit of knowledge or creative mastery is a spiritual vocation—writers, scholars, those engaged in serious magical practice, those facing questions that have no comfortable answers. He does not offer comfort. He offers clarity, at a price, and the price is usually some form of sacrifice—of certainty, of ease, of a version of yourself you were comfortable with.

Offerings to Óðinn traditionally include mead, poetry spoken aloud, and the raven as symbol. He is honored at crossroads and thresholds, in moments of decision, and in the darkness before understanding arrives. His sacred day in the modern Heathen week is Wednesday—Woden's day, his name preserved in the language without anyone noticing.

Thor

Domain: Thunder, protection, strength, agriculture, the common people.

Thor is the most approachable of the major gods—direct, physical, loyal, occasionally outwitted but never outworked. Where Óðinn is complex and morally ambiguous, Thor is consistent. He protects Miðgarðr. He shows up. He swings the hammer and goes home for dinner.

Practitioners drawn to Thor tend to value straightforwardness, physical or practical competence, and the kind of loyalty that does not require explanation. He is a god for those who work with their hands, who protect their families and communities without drama, who meet difficulty with effort rather than strategy.

Mjölnir is his symbol—worn as an amulet, displayed on an altar, used to bless ritual space in the same way it once blessed weddings and births. Offerings include ale, bread, and the work of one's hands. He is honored in storms, in physical labor, in moments of protection and defense. His day is Thursday—Thor's day, hidden in plain sight.

Freya

Domain: Love, desire, fertility, magic, war, death.

Freya is the most powerful goddess in the Norse pantheon, and the most frequently misunderstood. She is associated with love and beauty, yes—but also with seiðr, the most potent form of Norse magic, which she taught to Óðinn himself. She receives half of those who fall in battle. She weeps tears of gold. She is not soft.

Practitioners drawn to Freya tend to be those for whom passion—in any form—is a spiritual force: those engaged in magical practice, those navigating grief or desire, those who understand that love and death are not opposites but neighbors. She demands full engagement with life, not moderation.

Offerings include amber, gold jewelry, flowers, mead, and the first fruits of whatever creative or emotional labor you are bringing to fruition. She is honored at times of love and loss alike, and in any serious magical working. Cats are her sacred animal. Friday—Freya's day—is hers.

Freyr

Domain: Fertility, abundance, sunshine, rain, peace, sexuality.

65

Where Freya is passion, Freyr is abundance—the warmth that makes things grow, the ease that follows effort, the pleasure that is also sacred. He gave away his sword for love, a sacrifice that will cost him his life at Ragnarök. He accepted that cost. This willingness to trade power for connection is the defining note of his character.

Practitioners drawn to Freyr tend to value the rhythms of the natural world, the pleasures of the body, and the kind of generosity that gives without calculating the return. He is particularly honored in agricultural contexts, at harvest, and at the seasonal transitions of the year.

Offerings include grain, fruit, boar meat, and mead. The boar is his sacred animal. He responds to gratitude—for abundance already received as much as for abundance requested.

Frigg

Domain: Marriage, motherhood, household, fate, foresight.

Frigg is Óðinn's equal in the one way that matters most: she can see all of fate and chooses, deliberately, not to speak of what she knows. This restraint is her power, not a limitation on it. She is the keeper of things that are known but not said—the quiet knowledge that holds a household, a family, a community together.

Practitioners drawn to Frigg tend to be those who carry responsibility for others, who understand leadership as service, who find the sacred in the daily work of maintaining a home and a community. She is a goddess for parents, for those who grieve, for those who hold things together when holding together is the hardest possible task.

Offerings include fiber and thread—spinning and weaving were historically her domain—along with hearth offerings and the naming of the dead at seasonal gatherings. She is honored in the domestic sphere, at the threshold of the home, and in any ritual that concerns the welfare of children or family.

Loki

Domain: Change, disruption, cunning, boundaries, transformation.

Loki is the most contested figure in modern Heathenry, and the debate about his place in practice is real and ongoing. He is not evil—the Norse tradition had no simple Satan figure—but he is a force of disruption that produces both catastrophe and innovation, sometimes in the same moment. That combination makes him dangerous in ways that demand honest reckoning rather than casual dismissal.

Practitioners drawn to Loki tend to be those who are comfortable with contradiction, who have experienced the creative potential of chaos, who find that their own lives resist easy categorization. He is associated with change that cannot be controlled—the kind that strips away what is no longer serving you, whether you were ready to let it go or not.

Many kindreds do not honor Loki formally. Others maintain a relationship with him cautiously. Both positions are defensible within the tradition. What he demands, above all, is honesty—about who you are, about what you have done, about the parts of yourself you would prefer not to acknowledge.

Tyr

Domain: Justice, law, honorable combat, sacrifice for the greater good.

Tyr placed his sword hand in the wolf's mouth and lost it, accepting the cost of keeping the world safe without flinching and without complaint. He is the god for whom justice and sacrifice are not opposites but expressions of the same commitment. He lost his hand. He did not lose his word.

Practitioners drawn to Tyr tend to hold justice as a core value—those in legal professions, those engaged in advocacy, those who have had to make costly decisions in order to do what was right. He is honored when difficult but necessary choices must be made, when oaths are sworn, and when the cost of integrity becomes clear.

Offerings include justice enacted—a wrong corrected, a difficult truth spoken—alongside more traditional offerings of mead and oath-rings. Tuesday is Tyr's day.

Heimdallr

Domain: Vigilance, boundaries, community, the bridge between worlds.

Heimdallr stands at the boundary between Ásgarðr and everything else, watching, listening, waiting. He is the god of thresholds—the one who sees what is coming before it arrives, who guards the liminal spaces where one thing becomes another. He sleeps less than a bird and hears more than anyone.

Practitioners drawn to Heimdallr tend to be those who serve protective or watchful roles in their communities, those engaged in divination or prophetic work, and those who feel themselves drawn to the boundary spaces of life—beginnings and endings, transitions, the moment before change.

Offerings include mead and the simple act of paying attention—of slowing down enough to notice what is actually present rather than what you expect to find.

The Smaller Gods

Baldr — God of light, purity, and the world reborn. Honored in grief and in the gradual return of hope. Offerings of white flowers and light.

Njörðr — God of the sea, seafaring, fishing, and coastal prosperity. Honored by those who work on or near water, and in any rite concerned with abundance and fair weather. Offerings of fish and salt water.

Skaði — Goddess of winter, hunting, mountains, and independence. Her story is worth knowing in more detail than most of the figures in this section, because it says something distinctive about how the Norse pantheon actually worked. She arrived in Ásgarðr not as a supplicant but as a claimant, armed and demanding restitution for her father's death. The gods did not turn her away. They negotiated. She won the right to choose a husband from among the Æsir, received compensation for her loss, and was made to laugh—against her will, and against the gravity of the occasion—by Loki's absurdity. She chose Njörðr as her husband, and the marriage failed, as the sea and the mountains were always going to fail to accommodate each other. She returned to her peaks. She remained a goddess. Her story is less about defeat than about the terms on which a powerful figure from outside the divine order enters it—and the fact that those terms were hers to set. Honored by those who value solitude, self-reliance, and the particular clarity that comes from cold and altitude. Offerings of game meat and the bones of prey.

Bragi — God of poetry, eloquence, and the spoken word. Honored before any creative undertaking, at sumbel when the cup passes, and in any ritual that involves formal speech. Offerings of mead poured before a performance or recitation.

Iðunn — Goddess of youth, renewal, and the apples that keep the gods vital. Honored in spring, in recovery from illness, and whenever renewal after loss is needed. Offerings of apples and fresh growth.

Ullr — God of winter, archery, skiing, and the solitary hunt. Thor's stepson and a deity of considerable ancient importance, now honored primarily by those who practice winter sports or who feel drawn to the stillness of cold landscapes. Offerings of carved yew and the practiced skill of one's chosen discipline.

Víðarr — The silent god, god of vengeance and survival. One of the few to survive Ragnarök. Honored in silence, in the slow work of recovery after catastrophic loss, and by those who have outlasted something that was meant to destroy them.

Hel — Ruler of the realm of the dead, daughter of Loki. Misread by popular culture as a villain, she keeps her realm with consistency and fairness—most of the dead, after all, end up in her care. Honored at ancestor rites, at funerals, and in any practice that involves working with grief or the memory of the dead.

Sif — Goddess of grain, harvest, and the earth's fertility. Thor's wife and a figure whose golden hair connects her to the ripened fields of autumn. Honored at harvest time and in any domestic ritual concerned with abundance. Offerings of bread and grain.

Gefjon — Goddess of agriculture, abundance, and unmarried women. Her myth of plowing an entire kingdom into the sea in a single day marks her as a figure of formidable creative power operating on her own terms. Honored in any work that reshapes the land or the self.

Finding Your Fulltrúi

There is no formal process for identifying your fulltrúi. It tends to announce itself through repetition—a god whose stories keep finding you, whose symbols appear without you placing them there, whose domain maps precisely onto the central challenge or passion of your life at a particular time.

Start by working with the deities whose domains most clearly intersect with who you are and what you are engaged with. Make offerings consistently. Pay attention to what changes. A relationship with a god deepens the same way any relationship deepens—through patient, honest attention over time.

What this looks like in practice varies considerably from person to person. For some, the recognition arrives early and clearly—a particular myth lands with unexpected force, a symbol keeps surfacing, a deity's domain describes your life so precisely that the connection feels less like a choice than an acknowledgment of something already true. For others, it emerges gradually through the work itself: you begin making offerings to the god whose domain is most relevant to where you are, and over months of consistent practice, something in the relationship shifts from obligation to genuine familiarity.

Either way, the fulltrúi relationship is not static. It tends to intensify during the periods of your life that most directly engage that deity's domain, and to recede somewhat when circumstances change. A practitioner who builds a close relationship with Óðinn during years of intense study or creative work may find that relationship becoming less central during a period focused on family and community, where Frigg or Thor speaks more directly to what is actually happening. This is not inconsistency. It is the tradition working as it was always meant to—as a living framework that meets you where you are rather than demanding you conform to a fixed devotional identity.

The gods of Asatru do not require belief as a condition of approach. They require practice. Show up, make the offering, speak the name. Everything else follows from that.

Chapter 8

The Nine Noble Virtues

E very serious spiritual tradition eventually confronts the same question: how should a person live? Sacred texts and mythological stories can inspire, but inspiration without practical guidance leaves a gap between belief and behavior that most people find difficult to bridge on their own.

Asatru addresses this through a set of values known as the Nine Noble Virtues—Courage, Truth, Discipline, Fidelity, Honor, Hospitality, Industriousness, Self-Reliance, and Perseverance. These nine principles function as a practical ethical framework, a way of translating the values implicit in the Eddas and sagas into daily conduct.

Before working with them, though, it is worth knowing where they actually come from—because the Nine Noble Virtues are not ancient. They were codified in the 1970s, primarily through the work of figures associated with the Odinic Rite in Britain, as part of the broader effort to reconstruct a coherent modern Heathen practice. They draw on themes genuinely present throughout the old literature—the Hávamál in particular, Odin's collection of practical and philosophical wisdom, is saturated with these values—but the specific list of nine, in this form, is a modern synthesis.

This distinction matters for the same reason all such distinctions matter in Asatru: intellectual honesty about the sources is a form of integrity. The Nine Noble Virtues are valuable not because they are ancient but because they are well-grounded. They reflect something real about how the pre-Christian Norse understood the relationship between personal conduct and communal health. Used thoughtfully, they remain one of the most practical tools modern Heathenry has produced.

One additional note before we begin: in Asatru, virtues are never purely private. The web of wyrd—the interconnected fabric of fate explored in Chapter 4—means that every action a person takes ripples outward through their community and beyond. These nine values are not personal self-improvement goals. They are the qualities that make a person a trustworthy participant in the shared life of a kindred and, through the kindred, in the broader human community.

Courage

The Hávamál is direct on this point: "The cowardly man thinks he will live forever if he avoids battle, but old age gives him no peace, even if the spears spare him." Courage comes first among the Nine Noble Virtues because without it, none of the others can be practiced consistently. A person who lacks courage will find reasons—usually convincing ones—to set aside every other value when the cost of holding to it becomes apparent.

The relevant test of courage, for most practitioners today, rarely involves physical danger. It shows up instead in smaller and more persistent forms: the willingness to hold to an unpopular position, to acknowledge a mistake publicly, to maintain religious identity in environments that regard it as strange or suspect, to tell someone a truth they would prefer not to hear.

Tyr is the model here. He placed his hand in the wolf's mouth knowing what would follow, because the alternative—a cosmos unprotected from Fenrir—was worse than the loss of a hand. Courage in the Asatru tradition carries this structure: a clear-eyed assessment of what something costs, followed by the decision to pay that cost anyway, because the thing being protected is worth more than the comfort of avoiding the price.

This has nothing to do with recklessness. The sagas consistently distinguish between courage and foolhardiness. A warrior who charges into a battle he cannot win serves no one. Courage requires judgment—an accurate understanding of what you are facing—before it requires action.

Truth

The Norse tradition placed unusual weight on the spoken word. An oath, once made, was a binding commitment enforced not by legal structures but by personal honor and community recognition. To speak falsely was to devalue your own word, and a person whose word could not be trusted was, in the most practical sense, useless to their community.

Truth in this context has two dimensions. The first is straightforward honesty in daily life—saying what you mean, keeping what you promise, refusing to create impressions you know to be false. The Hávamál counsels: "Better not to pray than to offer too much; a gift always looks for a return. Better not to send than to send too much." The logic is the same—do not commit to what you cannot deliver, because the gap between your word and your action is the measure of your unreliability.

The second dimension is harder. Asatru asks its practitioners to pursue truth about themselves—their actual motivations, their real strengths and weaknesses, the places where they fall short of the values they profess. This kind of honesty has no audience and no social reward. It is practiced alone, in the sober assessment of whether you actually did what you said you would, whether you held to your values when holding to them was inconvenient, whether the person you present to your community reflects the person you actually are.

Odin's endless pursuit of wisdom—the eye surrendered, the nine days on the tree, the consultation of Mímir's severed head—is in part a myth about what the pursuit of truth actually costs. It is not a comfortable process, and it does not end.

Discipline

Self-discipline is the mechanism by which the other virtues function. Knowing what is right and doing what is right are different things, and the gap between them is where discipline lives.

In the Asatru context, discipline applies most visibly to religious practice itself. The reconstruction of a living faith from fragmentary sources, across a gap of a thousand years, requires dedicated and patient effort. Reading the Eddas and the sagas is not a one-time project. Developing a meaningful ritual practice takes time, repetition, and the willingness to continue through periods when the practice feels dry or unrewarding. Building relationships within a kindred demands the discipline of showing up consistently, of contributing reliably, of prioritizing the community's needs alongside your own.

The Hávamál is particularly direct about the discipline of moderation—in eating, in drinking, in speech, in the display of emotion. This is not puritanism. It is the practical observation that a person who cannot govern their own appetites and impulses will find it difficult to govern anything else, including their conduct toward others.

Discipline is also what prevents the pursuit of individual virtue from becoming self-absorption. A person with discipline keeps their commitments even when enthusiasm has faded. They complete what they started. They return to practice after they have failed at it, without excessive self-reproach and without abandoning the standard.

Fidelity

Fidelity means loyalty—to people, to commitments, to the tradition itself. In the Norse world, the bonds between individuals were the basic unit of social order. There was no abstract institution to appeal to when things went wrong. What existed instead was the network of personal obligations that connected people to one another, and the reliability of that network depended entirely on whether individuals honored their part of it.

Within a kindred, fidelity means reliability—showing up, following through, maintaining your commitments to the people who have made commitments to you. In personal relationships, it means the same thing the tradition has always meant: keeping your word, maintaining your bonds, not abandoning people when doing so would be convenient.

In relation to the gods, fidelity takes on an additional dimension. The Profession—the ritual act by which some Asatruar formally dedicate themselves to their practice—is understood as a relationship entered into voluntarily and maintained with the same seriousness as any other significant commitment. You honor the gods by returning to practice consistently, by keeping the seasonal festivals, by maintaining the altar even when nothing dramatic is happening. Fidelity in this sense is the opposite of spiritual tourism—the restless movement from tradition to tradition that mistakes novelty for depth.

The tradition also values fidelity to history. Understanding what the pre-Christian Norse actually believed and practiced, rather than substituting more comfortable modern assumptions, is itself a form of loyalty—to the ancestors whose tradition is being reconstructed.

Honor

Honor is at the center of the Asatru ethical system, and it operates differently from how the concept tends to function in modern Western culture. In the Norse tradition, honor was an internal quality—the alignment between what you professed to value and how you actually behaved—not a social credential managed for external approval.

The sagas are populated by figures whose honor is their defining characteristic. We remember them because they held to their values under pressure, at cost, without the guarantee of recognition or reward. We also remember those who did not—whose names remain attached to betrayal and cowardice across a thousand years of oral and written tradition. The Norse understood reputation as a long game, played across generations, and they took it seriously accordingly.

The Hávamál puts it plainly: "Cattle die, kinsmen die, the self must also die; but the glory of reputation never dies, for the man who achieves it." This is not vanity. It is an acknowledgment that how a person lived—the quality of their choices under pressure—outlasts the physical person and continues to affect the world they left behind.

Inner honor and outer reputation are related but separate. A person can have a strong reputation built on false impressions, and a person can act with real honor in circumstances where no one is watching and no recognition will follow. Asatru consistently prioritizes the inner reality. Honor refers to what you know to be true about yourself, in the moments when no one is watching and there is no social benefit to doing the right thing.

Hospitality

Hospitality was among the most fundamental obligations in pre-Christian Norse culture, and its importance is not difficult to understand in context. In a world without reliable institutions, without hotels or legal protections for travelers, without the infrastructure that modern people take for granted, the willingness of one household to receive a stranger was literally a matter of survival. The guest who could not find shelter might die. The host who turned away a traveler in need violated a code that the entire community depended on.

The mythological grounding for this is unusually direct. Odin travels the world in disguise—a tired old man, a wandering stranger—testing the hospitality of those he encounters. The gods visit human households incognito. The stranger at the door might be more than a stranger. This is not simply a theological claim. It is an ethical instruction: treat everyone who comes to you with real need as someone whose dignity demands a response.

In modern Asatru communities, hospitality takes practical forms that have little to do with providing shelter for travelers. It shows up in the willingness to make newcomers feel welcome at rituals and gatherings, in the pooling of resources within a kindred when a member faces difficulty, in the basic practice of treating people—regardless of their background or belief—with the dignity that the tradition insists on.

Hospitality also implies reciprocity. The Norse tradition was clear that the gift relationship—the exchange of generosity—was not one-directional. A community of people who only give, or only receive, is out of balance. The virtue lies in participating honestly in both directions.

Industriousness

The Hávamál has little patience for idleness. It praises the person who rises early, who maintains their property and their skills, who contributes to their community through consistent and capable effort. The Vikings, whatever else they were, were extraordinarily productive people—builders, traders, farmers, craftspeople, explorers—and the tradition reflects this orientation toward active engagement with the world.

Industriousness in the Asatru context means bringing real effort to whatever you are doing—your work, your practice, your community relationships, your creative and intellectual development. Half-measures are not honored. The gods are not impressed by intentions that do not result in action, by projects begun and abandoned, by the endless planning that substitutes for the work itself.

This virtue also applies to the practice of Asatru itself. Reconstructing a living tradition from fragmentary sources is demanding work. Learning Old Norse, studying the primary texts, developing ritual competence, building relationships within a kindred—none of this happens passively. The tradition rewards the practitioner who puts in the work, not with supernatural results necessarily, but with the kind of depth and rootedness that only long-term effort produces.

Self-Reliance

The Asatru relationship with the gods is one of the most theologically distinctive aspects of the tradition, and self-reliance is central to understanding it. Asatruar do not kneel. They stand. This is not arrogance—it is a statement about the nature of the relationship being sought. The gods are not asked for rescue from consequences the practitioner has created. They are approached as allies, as senior partners in a shared project, by someone who has already done what they could do for themselves.

Self-reliance in this sense means taking responsibility for your own life—your choices, their consequences, and the work of addressing what needs to be addressed. The Norse tradition had little patience for the displacement of personal responsibility onto forces outside the self. What happens to you is partly a matter of fate, yes—the Norns weave, and no one escapes wyrd. But how you respond to what happens is yours entirely, and the tradition is consistent in placing the highest value on responses that involve courage, effort, and the refusal to be diminished by difficulty.

This does not mean isolation or the rejection of community. The sagas are full of people who support one another through hardship, who lend their skills and their resources to those who need them. Self-reliance coexists with hospitality precisely because neither can function without the other. A community of people who each carry their own weight is one where hospitality is given freely, rather than extracted by need.

Perseverance

The Norse worldview offers no guarantees. The gods will fight at Ragnarök and they will lose. The cosmos will end, and begin again, without consulting anyone's preferences about the timing. What the tradition does offer—consistently, across the mythology, the sagas, and the practical wisdom of the Hávamál—is a model for how to behave in the face of difficulty and loss.

Perseverance means continuing. After the kindred dissolves. After the project fails. After the practice feels empty for weeks and the gods seem silent. After you have failed at the very virtue you were working on and must begin again. The Hávamál counsels patience and endurance not as passive resignation but as active choices—the decision to stay engaged, to keep working, to refuse to be defeated by what has not yet been resolved.

The Einherjar in Valhalla fight every day and die every day and return every night to feast and begin again. This is not a pleasant image, but it is an honest one. The work of building a life of honor, of maintaining relationships and practice and community, is repetitive and often unglamorous. Perseverance is what makes it possible over time.

The person who eventually achieves something difficult—who builds a lasting kindred, who masters a skill, who recovers from a significant loss and rebuilds—did not succeed because the path was easy. They succeeded because they kept going after the point where stopping seemed reasonable.

Living the Virtues

The Nine Noble Virtues are most useful when treated as a practice rather than a checklist. Reading about courage is not the same as noticing, in a specific moment, that you are avoiding something because it is uncomfortable, and choosing differently. The virtues become real through their application in ordinary life—in the small decisions that accumulate into character over time.

Many Asatruar use the Hávamál as a companion text to the NNV, reading it slowly and returning to it across years of practice. Its wisdom is practical, sometimes blunt, occasionally surprising, and consistently rooted in the same values the Nine Noble Virtues articulate. Working with both together—the modern framework and the ancient text—gives the ethical practice of Asatru both clarity and depth.

The goal, in the end, is not perfection in any of the nine virtues. It is the ongoing, honest effort to live in a way that you can account for—to yourself, to your community, and to the tradition you are part of. In Asatru, we are our deeds. The virtues are the measure by which those deeds are made.

Chapter 9

Norse Magic: Seiðr, Shamanism, and the Runes

The Norse cosmos, as the previous chapters have made clear, was not a passive backdrop to human life. It was alive—inhabited, layered, and accessible to those who knew how to move through it. The gods traveled between worlds. The dead remained connected to the living. The Norns wove fate from a well at the base of the World Tree. Against this backdrop, it would have been strange if the people of pre-Christian Scandinavia had not developed sophisticated methods for engaging with the forces that surrounded them—methods for reaching across the boundary between the ordinary world and the sacred one, for reading the threads of fate before they pulled tight, for drawing on powers larger than the individual self.

They developed several such methods. Two stand at the center of the magical tradition that modern Asatru has inherited: seiðr, the shamanic practice of spirit-travel and fate-working, and the runes, the sacred alphabet through which the deepest forces of the cosmos could be named, invoked, and worked with. The two practices are distinct but not separate—both draw on the same fundamental understanding that the universe is saturated with meaning, and that meaning can be engaged with directly by those with the skill and the preparation to do so.

This chapter introduces both.

Óðinn and the Shamanic Inheritance

Any account of Norse magic begins with Óðinn, because Óðinn is the divine model for every major magical practice the tradition contains.

His name tells you something essential. Óðr—the root from which Óðinn derives—means ecstasy, fury, inspiration, the state of consciousness that exceeds ordinary waking awareness. Óðinn is, in the most literal etymological sense, the master of that state. Everything he does magically flows from his willingness to enter it: the nine days hanging on Yggdrasil, the eye dropped into Mímir's well, the ravens sent out each morning to gather what the waking world cannot see. These are not metaphors. They are descriptions of a technology—a set of practices for accessing knowledge that ordinary consciousness cannot reach.

This technology has a name shared across Eurasian cultures: shamanism. Though the word itself comes from the Tungusic peoples of Siberia, the practices it describes—spirit-travel through altered states, communication with ancestors and non-human beings, the use of ritual to cross the boundary between the ordinary world and the sacred one—appear throughout the Norse tradition with enough consistency and specificity to constitute a recognizable shamanic complex.

The Ynglinga Saga records that Óðinn could travel to distant lands while his body lay still, appearing to be asleep or dead. He rode Sleipnir, his eight-legged horse—a figure that appears across northern Eurasian shamanism as the classic vehicle for journeys to the underworld. He sent his ravens Huginn and Muninn, thought and memory, as extensions of his consciousness into the Nine Worlds each day. He descended to Helheim to consult a dead seeress about his son's prophetic dreams. Every element of the classic shamanic profile is present: the altered state, the spirit helpers, the underworld journey, the capacity to mediate between the living and the dead.

That the chief god of the Norse pantheon was also its supreme shaman tells you something important about how the tradition valued these practices. Magic in the Norse world was not peripheral. It was at the center.

Seiðr: The Art of Weaving Fate

Seiðr (pronounced roughly "SAY-thr") was the primary Norse magical practice, and its defining characteristic was its relationship to fate. Where many magical traditions attempt to produce specific outcomes through will and ritual, seiðr operated at a more fundamental level—it worked with the threads of fate themselves, reading what the Norns had woven and, in the hands of a sufficiently skilled practitioner, symbolically weaving new possibilities into the existing fabric.

The primary practitioners of seiðr were women known as völur (singular völva)—seeresses who traveled between communities, performing their work in exchange for food, shelter, and payment. The Saga of Erik the Red contains the most detailed account of a völva at work: she arrives at a farmstead dressed in a cloak of black lambskin lined with cat fur, wearing a hood of black lambskin lined with white catskin, carrying a staff topped with a brass knob set with stones. She is seated on a high platform, and the community gathers to sing the traditional songs—varðlokur, ward-songs—that call the spirits to attend. From that elevated seat, in a state of trance, she answers the questions of the community: what the coming season will bring, where game can be found, what fate holds for specific individuals.

The völva was understood to travel in spirit through the Nine Worlds while her body remained on the platform. What she encountered there—gods, spirits, ancestors, the Norns themselves—was the source of the knowledge she brought back. The practice had clear parallels to shamanic traditions across northern Eurasia: the elevated seat, the spirit helpers called by song, the trance journey, the return with information or healing.

Seiðr carried a significant social complexity for men who practiced it. The association between seiðr and weaving—a fundamentally feminine domain in Norse culture—meant that male practitioners risked being labeled argr (unmanly), one of the most serious social insults available. Yet Óðinn himself was a seiðr practitioner, having learned the art from Freya, and even he was occasionally taunted with the accusation. The existence of this paradox—the most powerful god practicing what was considered a feminizing art—suggests a tradition comfortable with the kind of boundary-crossing that power sometimes requires. Some of the most capable people in any tradition work in spaces that resist easy categorization.

Seiðr continues as a living practice in modern Asatru, though its revival has required careful reconstruction from fragmentary sources. Contemporary practitioners typically work in groups, with one person taking the seer's role on an elevated seat while others maintain the ritual container through song, drumming, or structured meditation. The questions brought to a seiðr working tend to reflect the same concerns as those in the sagas: community wellbeing, personal guidance, communication with ancestors. The technology is ancient. The questions it addresses are perennial.

The Berserkers: Shamanism in Battle

Seiðr was not the only form the Norse shamanic inheritance took. Among warriors, ecstatic practice found a very different expression in the berserkir (bear-shirts) and úlfheðnar (wolf-hides)—fighters who entered a state of battle-trance so complete that they were said to be impervious to iron and fire, possessed by the spirit of their totem animal, fused with the divine fury of Óðinn himself.

The Ynglinga Saga describes them: Óðinn's men went into battle without armor, mad as dogs or wolves, biting their shields, slaying men while neither fire nor iron could harm them. This was not metaphor—or not only metaphor. The berserker tradition involved real initiatory practice, ritual preparation, and the deliberate cultivation of an altered state that modern scholars have associated with everything from animal shamanism to psychoactive substances to the specific neurological state of combat dissociation.

What matters for understanding Norse magic is the underlying principle: that the boundary between the human self and larger forces—divine, animal, cosmic—was permeable, and that skilled practitioners could deliberately dissolve it in service of a specific purpose. The völva dissolved that boundary to receive knowledge. The berserker dissolved it to become a weapon. Both drew on the same fundamental cosmological understanding—that the ordinary human self is one configuration among many, and that other configurations are accessible through the right preparation and the right state of mind.

The Runes: Letters That Are Also Forces

Alongside seiðr, the runes constitute the other great magical inheritance of the Norse tradition—and unlike seiðr, they have left a physical record that spans more than a thousand years of continuous use across northern Europe.

The word rún (plural rúnar) meant, in Old Norse, both "letter" and "secret" or "mystery." This double meaning is the key to understanding what runes actually were in the pre-Christian world. They were not simply an alphabet—though they functioned as one. They were understood as forces, as cosmic principles that had always existed and were waiting to be discovered rather than invented. Each rune named something real about the structure of the universe, and to carve or speak a rune was to engage directly with that force.

The myth of their origin makes this explicit. Óðinn did not invent the runes. He found them—through the same process of sacrificial self-diminishment that runs through every account of his acquisition of knowledge. He hung on Yggdrasil for nine days and nights, wounded by his own spear, without food or drink, gazing down into the void beneath the World Tree. On the ninth night, the runes revealed themselves. He screamed, seized them, and fell back to earth.

The cost was nine days of ordeal. What he received in return was access to the deepest language the cosmos possesses.

The Elder Futhark

Three main runic systems developed across the Germanic world, of which the Elder Futhark is the oldest and the one most widely used in modern Asatru practice. Its name comes from the sounds of its first six runes—Fehu, Uruz, Thurisaz, Ansuz, Raidho, Kenaz—in the same way that "alphabet" derives from alpha and beta. It contains twenty-four runes, divided into three groups of eight (ættir), and was in use across the Germanic world until approximately 700 CE, when it began to shift into the simplified Younger Futhark of the Viking Age.

What follows is a working introduction to each of the twenty-four runes—their traditional meanings, their divinatory associations, and the forces they represent. This is material to return to over time, not to absorb in a single reading.

Fehu ᚠ — Wealth, cattle, mobile resources. The rune of abundance that moves and circulates. In a reading, it speaks to financial matters, to the energy of acquisition and responsible stewardship of what you have.

Uruz ᚢ — Aurochs, primal strength. The wild ox, undomesticated and untameable. Uruz represents raw vital force—the power that cannot be owned or controlled, only channeled. Associated with health, endurance, and the strength to overcome obstacles.

Thurisaz ᚦ — Giant, thorn. The force of directed, concentrated power. In mythology, thurisaz connects to the Jötnar—the giants—and to Thor's hammer. Protective in the right hands, destructive when misapplied. In a reading it warns of forces that require careful handling.

Ansuz ᚨ — God, divine breath. The rune of Óðinn, of inspired speech and divine communication. Associated with language, poetry, prophecy, and the reception of wisdom from beyond the ordinary self. When Ansuz appears, pay attention to what is being communicated.

Raidho ⟩ — Riding, journey. Focused motion toward a goal. Raidho speaks to travel, but also to the alignment of effort and direction—the difference between movement and purposeful movement. In a reading, it asks whether you are moving in the right direction.

Kenaz ⟨ — Torch, ulcer. The controlled fire that illuminates. Kenaz is the light of knowledge, craft, and creative work—the fire that serves rather than destroys. Associated with learning, skill, and the clarity that comes from careful, ongoing attention.

Gebo ⟨ — Gift. The sacred exchange. In Norse culture, gifts created bonds—between people, between humans and gods. Gebo speaks to reciprocity, to the relationships maintained through giving and receiving, and to the sacred nature of generosity.

Wunjo ⟨ — Joy, harmony. The rune of wellbeing and right relationship. Wunjo speaks to the satisfaction that comes when things are in alignment—with your values, your community, your deepest purposes. Its appearance in a reading suggests either the presence of such harmony or the direction toward it.

Hagalaz ⟨ — Hail. Disruption from outside your control. The hailstone destroys the harvest but melts into water that nourishes the next planting. Hagalaz represents sudden, unavoidable change—difficult in the moment, potentially transformative over time.

Naudhiz ⟨ — Need, necessity. The friction of constraint. Naudhiz speaks to the places where want and reality do not align, but also to the determination that such friction can produce. Resistance, in this rune's understanding, generates the force needed to break through it.

Isa ⟨ — Ice. Stillness, stasis, the pause that cannot be rushed. Isa does not promise progress. It counsels patience—the understanding that some things must wait until conditions change, and that forcing movement before the ice melts is futile.

Jera ⁜ — Year, harvest. The cycle completed. Jera speaks to the reward of patient effort—the harvest that comes in its own time, neither rushed nor delayed. Associated with the natural rhythms of the year and the trust that right action eventually produces right results.

Eihwaz ⁜ — Yew tree. The tree that lives longest, whose wood makes the bow, whose roots reach deepest. Eihwaz is the rune of Yggdrasil—of endurance, of the axis that holds things together, of the transformation that comes at endings. Associated with magic, protection, and the crossing of thresholds.

Perthro ⁜ — The lot-cup, hidden things. The rune of chance, of what is concealed, of fate not yet revealed. Perthro speaks to the uncertainty that underlies all human planning and to the wisdom of engaging with that uncertainty honestly rather than pretending to certainty you do not have.

Elhaz ⁜ — Elk-sedge, defense. One of the most powerful protective runes. Elhaz speaks to the instinct for self-protection and the protection of those in your care—the reaching gesture that holds danger at bay.

Sowulo ⁜ — Sun. The power of clarity, vitality, and directed will. Sowulo is the force that cuts through confusion, that energizes and illuminates. Associated with success, health, and the confident purposefulness that comes from knowing what you stand for.

Teiwaz ⁜ — Tyr. Justice, honorable sacrifice, the willingness to pay the necessary cost. Teiwaz carries the same meaning as Tyr's myth—the hand in the wolf's mouth, the loss accepted in service of something greater. Associated with legal matters, with moral courage, and with the discipline of holding to your values under pressure.

Berkana ⁜ — Birch tree. New growth, birth, the beginning of a cycle. Berkana speaks to fertility in its broadest sense—the emergence of new life, new projects, new phases of development. Its energy is gentle but persistent, like spring growth pushing through frozen ground.

Ehwaz ▯ — Horse. The partnership between rider and mount—mutual trust, the harmony of two moving together toward a shared goal. Ehwaz speaks to relationships, to the power of real collaboration, and to the smooth flow that comes when two forces are fully aligned.

Mannaz ▯ — Human being. The rune of humanity in its fullest sense—the capacity for reason, for self-reflection, for the kind of conscious action that distinguishes human choices from mere instinct. Associated with intelligence, with community, and with the honest assessment of your own nature.

Laguz ▯ — Water, lake. The power of flow, of depth, of the unconscious and the intuitive. Laguz speaks to the knowledge that lies below the surface of ordinary awareness and to the wisdom of moving with the natural current rather than against it.

Inguz ▯ — Freyr, fertility. The contained potential that releases when the time is right. Inguz speaks to gestation, to the energy that builds quietly before expressing itself fully. Associated with Freyr and the fertility of the earth, with hearth and home, and with the protective warmth of the family circle.

Dagaz ▯ — Day. The moment of breakthrough, the threshold between darkness and light. Dagaz carries the energy of transformation—the sudden shift when one condition gives way to another, rather than gradual erosion. It is the rune of the tipping point, the dawn.

Othala ▯ — Ancestral home, inherited wealth. The rune of what is passed down—land, bloodline, culture, the accumulated wisdom and luck of those who came before. Othala speaks to ancestry, to the responsibility of inheritance, and to the wealth that belongs to a lineage rather than an individual.

Working with the Runes

The runes can be engaged with in several ways, each suited to different purposes and different levels of practice.

Divination is the most accessible entry point. A simple three-rune cast—drawn from a bag, placed left to right—can speak to the past forces shaping a situation, the present dynamic, and the direction in which things are moving. A nine-rune cast, drawn all at once and scattered on a cloth, allows for a more complex reading in which position and orientation add layers of meaning. The key in either case is to begin with a clear question, to approach the runes with real openness rather than a preferred answer, and to work with what appears even when—especially when—it is not what you hoped to see.

Meditation on individual runes develops a direct experiential relationship with the forces they represent, beyond what any written description can convey. Many practitioners spend a week or more with a single rune, carving it, carrying it, noticing where it appears in daily life, and working with it in quiet contemplation before moving to the next. Over twenty-four weeks, this practice builds a relationship with the entire Futhark that no amount of reading can substitute for.

Making your own rune set is considered important in many Heathen traditions, precisely because of the connection formed through the process of creation. A set carved from a fallen branch, or painted on river stones, or pressed into clay—made with attention and intention—carries a different quality than one purchased ready-made. The material matters less than the care. The act of making is itself a form of magical engagement.

Galdr—the practice of chanting or intoning the rune names—is among the oldest forms of runic magic. The sound of each rune's name resonates with the force the rune represents, and focused, repeated chanting can shift the practitioner's state of consciousness in ways that simple visualization cannot. This is advanced practice, best approached slowly and with grounding preparation.

What the Ordeal Was For

Both seiðr and runic practice share a fundamental orientation: the conviction that the cosmos is not indifferent to human engagement, that the forces which shape reality can be approached, and that the practitioner who develops the skill, the patience, and the willingness to pay the necessary cost of such engagement can genuinely participate in the fabric of existence rather than simply being carried along by it.

Óðinn hung on the tree because he believed what was waiting at the bottom of that ordeal was worth the price. The völva climbed onto her platform and opened herself to whatever the Nine Worlds chose to send because her community needed what she could bring back. The warrior who carved teiwaz on his blade before battle was doing the same thing at a smaller scale—calling on the force that the rune named, asking it to be present.

Those who engage with these practices today inherit that same orientation. The forms are reconstructed; the underlying impulse is continuous. Show up. Pay attention. Be willing to receive what actually comes rather than what you expected. Work with the forces as they are, not as you wish they were.

The runes have been waiting in the well at the base of the tree for a long time. They will still be there when you are ready to find them.

Chapter 10

Sacred Symbols of Asatru

S ymbols in the Norse tradition were never purely decorative. They were understood as concentrations of force—visible points where the power of the cosmos could be held, carried, displayed, and engaged with directly. When a Viking carved a symbol onto a weapon, a ship prow, or a piece of jewelry, the act was understood as an invocation: a deliberate drawing of specific forces into proximity with the person or object marked.

This understanding continues in modern Asatru. The symbols in this chapter are not museum pieces or aesthetic choices. They are tools—each one carrying a specific meaning, a specific set of associations, and a specific relevance to the practice of a living faith. Some are worn as amulets. Some are carved into ritual objects or displayed on altars. Some are drawn or visualized during meditation and magical working. All of them encode, in visual form, something important about the Norse cosmological understanding that the previous chapters have been building.

A note on overlaps: Yggdrasil and the runic alphabet are treated in depth in earlier chapters and appear here only briefly, in their function as symbols rather than cosmological or magical systems. Mjölnir is discussed in the context of Thor's worship in Chapter 7. The focus here is on the symbols that have not yet received their full due.

Mjölnir – Thunder and Lightning

The most widely recognized symbol in modern Heathenry needs only brief treatment here, given what Chapter 7 already covers. Mjölnir—Thor's hammer—functions in Asatru as a consecrating instrument, a protective amulet, and a statement of religious identity. More than fifty Mjölnir pendants have been recovered from Norse archaeological sites across Scandinavia and the British Isles, suggesting that wearing the hammer was as common in the Viking Age as wearing a cross was in medieval Europe—and carried similar meaning.

Practitioners wear Mjölnir for the same reasons their ancestors did: as an acknowledgment of Thor's protective presence, as a marker of belonging to the Heathen tradition, and as a physical anchor for the values the hammer represents—strength, reliability, the defense of those in one's care. Archaeological finds show Mjölnir pendants worn alongside Christian crosses, reflecting the polytheistic ease with which the Norse incorporated multiple sacred symbols into a single practice.

Vegvisir – The Viking Compass

The Vegvísir is a compass-like symbol composed of eight unique runic staves radiating from a central point. Its name translates as "wayfinder" or "sign post"—from vegur (way) and vísir (pointer)—and its traditional purpose was to ensure that the bearer would find their way through storms and difficult terrain, even when the path ahead was obscured.

The primary historical source for the Vegvísir is the seventeenth-century Icelandic manuscript known as the Galdrabók, a collection of magical spells compiled long after the Viking Age. This later dating has led some scholars to question how deep its roots run in the pre-Christian tradition, though its structural similarity to other protective stave-symbols suggests real continuity with older practice.

What distinguishes the Vegvísir from a simple compass symbol is its magical dimension. The eight staves are not directions in the geographical sense—they are protective forces, each one extending outward to guard the bearer against the disorientation that comes when circumstances conspire to obscure the way forward. In modern Asatru, the Vegvísir is used both as a physical amulet and as a meditation object—a visual reminder that the way exists even when it cannot currently be seen, and that the forces invoked in its symbol are present to assist in finding it.

It is frequently confused with the Aegishjálmr, to which it is visually related. The distinction matters: where the Vegvísir guides, the Aegishjálmr protects.

Aegishjalmr – Protection and Victory

Eight symmetrical arms radiate from the center of the Aegishjálmr, each one composed of crossed runes of protection and hardening. Unlike the unique arms of the Vegvísir, the Aegishjálmr's arms are identical—a mandala of pure, concentrated protective force, turned in all directions simultaneously.

The name translates as "helm of awe" or "helm of terror," and the Völsunga Saga records that the dragon Fáfnir wore it between his eyes to strike fear into his enemies and render himself impervious to attack. Sigurðr claimed it after killing the dragon. In other accounts, the symbol functions as a sphere of invisible protection that surrounds the bearer, creating an aura of presence that causes adversaries to hesitate.

In modern practice, the Aegishjálmr is drawn or carved in contexts requiring protection—on the threshold of a home, on ritual tools, on the body before any undertaking that involves real risk. Some practitioners trace it with one finger between their own eyes before a difficult confrontation or challenge, following the literal interpretation of Fáfnir's usage in the saga. The deeper meaning encoded in its structure—hardening runes crossed by protective ones, turned outward in every direction—is a statement about the kind of protection the Norse tradition valued most: not the avoidance of difficulty, but the cultivated inner resilience that makes difficulty bearable.

Valknut – Fallen Heroes

Three interlocking triangles, nine corners in total, form the Valknut—one of the most visually striking and cosmologically dense symbols in the Norse tradition. The name derives from valr (the slain in battle) and knut (knot), and it appears on several Viking Age runestones and memorial stones in direct association with Óðinn and with scenes of death and the afterlife.

The nine corners correspond to the Nine Worlds. The three triangles have been interpreted as representing the threefold nature of existence—past, present, and future; or the three levels of the World Tree; or the three tribes of divine beings (Æsir, Vanir, Jötnar) whose relationships structure the cosmos. The interlocking structure, in which each triangle passes through the others, speaks to the interconnection of all these elements—the impossibility of separating the strands once they have been woven together.

The Valknut's association with Óðinn and with the honored dead makes it a particularly appropriate symbol for ancestor veneration. Many practitioners place it on altars dedicated to those who have died, particularly those who died well—with courage, with their values intact, leaving something worth inheriting behind them. It appears as a symbol of transition, of the crossing from one state of being to another, and of Óðinn's role as the one who receives the dead and holds their memory.

Its power as a symbol comes precisely from its density—nine corners, three triangles, one figure, all of the Nine Worlds compressed into a shape that fits in the palm of a hand.

Triskele – The Horns of Odin

Three interlocking drinking horns form the Triskele, also called the Horns of Óðinn or the Triple Horn. The three horns—Óðrœrir, Boðn, and Són—are the three vessels into which the blood of Kvasir was drained when the dwarves created the Mead of Poetry. Óðinn eventually obtained the mead through three nights of bargaining and ingenuity, drinking from each horn in turn before escaping in the form of an eagle.

The symbol is therefore intimately connected with poetic inspiration, with the gift of eloquence, and with the transformative power that the Mead of Poetry represents—the capacity to speak in a way that changes something, that moves people, that carries more than ordinary meaning. Its appearance on the Larbro stone in Sweden and the Snoldelev stone in Denmark confirms its currency in the Viking Age, though its precise ritual use remains a matter of scholarly discussion.

The Triskele is particularly associated with those who work in creative fields—writers, poets, musicians, artists—who honor Óðinn in his aspect as the divine patron of inspiration. It appears on altars dedicated to creative practice, is worn by those seeking the clarity and eloquence that the Mead of Poetry represents, and is invoked before any act of serious creative work. The three-part structure also speaks to the threefold nature of time—past, present, and the becoming that connects them—placing creative work in its proper cosmological context.

Web of Wyrd – Past, Present, Future

Nine lines crossing one another in a specific pattern create the Web of Wyrd—a symbol that encodes all twenty-four runes of the Elder Futhark within a single figure. Each rune's shape can be found within the web, making it simultaneously the simplest and most complex symbol in the tradition: a single image that contains, in potential, everything that can be written or spoken in the runic alphabet.

The symbol's connection to wyrd—the fate that the Norns weave at the base of Yggdrasil—makes it a meditation object of unusual depth. To contemplate the Web of Wyrd is to contemplate the structure of fate itself: the way all things are connected, the way each thread of each life is part of a fabric that no individual can see in its entirety, the way past choices have already shaped the present and present choices are already shaping what is becoming.

There is no firm archaeological evidence that the Web of Wyrd was used as a symbol during the Viking Age—its modern form appears to be a relatively recent reconstruction, developed within contemporary Heathenry. This does not diminish its utility as a contemplative and meditative symbol, but practitioners who use it honestly should know its origins. What it represents—the interconnection of fate and the containment of all runic potential within a single figure—is deeply grounded in the tradition even if the specific visual form is not ancient.

Irminsul — The Sacred Pillar

The Irminsul is one of the oldest sacred symbols in the Germanic tradition, pre-dating the Viking Age and connecting the Norse world to the broader Indo-European religious heritage from which it emerged. The name comes from Old Saxon—Irmin (great, universal) and sul (pillar, column)—and it designates a sacred post or column that served as a physical representation of the world axis, the cosmic center around which all of existence revolves.

The most historically documented Irminsul was a great pillar at the Saxon holy site of Eresburg, destroyed by Charlemagne in 772 CE as part of his forced conversion of the Saxons—an act of deliberate iconoclasm that tells you something about how significant the symbol was to those who venerated it. Representations of the Irminsul typically show a stylized tree or column, sometimes with branches, sometimes with a circular element at the top representing the sky or the sun.

The Irminsul is Yggdrasil rendered in physical, architectural form—the axis between worlds made present in a specific location, consecrating that location as a meeting point between the human and the divine. In modern Asatru, carved or constructed Irminsul pillars are placed at ritual sites, serving the same function that the original did: marking the center, establishing the sacred axis, and grounding the practice in a specific, physical point where the worlds touch.

Sleipnir — The Eight-Legged Horse

Óðinn's horse Sleipnir is unusual among Norse sacred symbols in being a figure rather than an abstract design—and his eight legs are the key to his symbolic meaning. In shamanic traditions across northern Eurasia, the eight-legged horse is consistently associated with the transition between life and death, with the journey of the soul between worlds, and with the capacity of the shaman to move where ordinary human beings cannot.

Sleipnir was born from Loki's shapeshifting—Loki transformed himself into a mare to distract the giant's stallion during the construction of Ásgarðr's walls, and Sleipnir was the offspring of that unlikely union. He could travel by land, sea, and air, and could carry his rider to Helheim—as he carried Hermóðr on Óðinn's behalf when Baldr died. He is the fastest and most capable horse in the Nine Worlds precisely because he belongs fully to none of them.

As a symbol, Sleipnir represents the capacity for passage—between worlds, between states of being, between the known and the unknown. He is used as a symbol by those engaged in shamanic or trance work, by those navigating significant life transitions, and by travelers—literal and metaphorical—who need the assurance that the journey between where they are and where they need to be is possible, however difficult the terrain.

Svefnthorn — The Sleep Thorn

The Svefnthorn appears in several Norse sagas and in post-Viking Age magical manuscripts as a symbol with the power to induce a deep, unbreakable sleep—one from which the sleeper would not wake until the spell was lifted. In the Völsunga Saga, Óðinn uses it to put the Valkyrie Brynhildr into an enchanted sleep after she defies his will, surrounding her with a ring of fire that only Sigurðr will be able to cross.

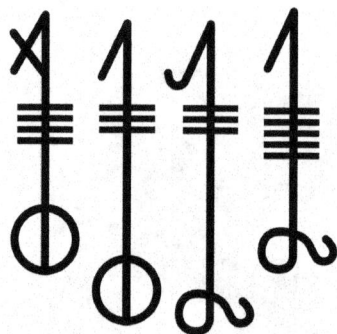

Its visual form varies significantly across sources—there is no single authoritative depiction—which suggests a symbol whose power was understood to inhere in the intention and knowledge of the practitioner rather than in one specific shape. Some sources show it as a series of stave-like projections; others as a more complex runic composition.

In modern practice, the Svefnthorn is associated with sleep, dreams, and the liminal state between waking and unconscious awareness—the threshold through which the Norse understanding of spirit-travel and prophetic dreaming passes. Some practitioners use versions of it in the context of seiðr work, as a symbol to facilitate the trance state. Others work with it in relation to healing sleep, to the resolution of conflict through a period of enforced stillness, or to the mythological theme of transformation that requires a period of apparent dormancy before the new state can emerge.

Carrying the Symbols

The question of which symbols to work with is ultimately a personal one, shaped by the specific relationship each practitioner is building with the tradition. A few principles are worth keeping in mind.

Wear what you understand. A symbol whose meaning you cannot explain—to yourself or to someone who asks—is not yet yours. Start with one or two symbols whose resonance is clear, and let the relationship with them deepen before adding others.

Make when possible. A symbol carved, painted, or forged by your own hands carries a different quality than one purchased. The process of making focuses attention on meaning in ways that acquisition cannot replicate. This is not a rule but an observation confirmed by centuries of practice.

Use them actively. These symbols are most powerful when engaged with intentionally—worn consciously, placed deliberately on an altar, carved with attention to what you are asking them to do. The difference between a symbol worn as decoration and one worn as a conscious invocation is the practitioner's awareness of what they are holding.

The Norse world was saturated with these forms of meaning. Every carving, every pendant, every mark on a doorpost was a small act of engagement with the forces the cosmos contains. Modern Asatru inherits that orientation—the understanding that the visible world and the sacred one are not separate, and that the symbols that connect them are worth carrying with care.

Chapter 11

Worship and Rituals

A satru makes an unusual claim about what religion is for. Most modern Western faiths locate the sacred primarily in belief—in the content of what you hold to be true. Asatru locates it primarily in practice—in what you do, repeatedly, with attention and intention, in relationship with the gods, the ancestors, and the living world around you.

This distinction has consequences. It means that the question "are you Asatru?" is answered less by what you believe about the cosmos than by whether you show up—whether you make the offerings, speak the names, maintain the altars, observe the seasonal rhythms, and participate in the communal rites that constitute a living tradition. Faith, in this framework, is something you build through action rather than something you hold in private.

This chapter covers the primary forms that Asatru worship takes: the sacred spaces in which it occurs, the two central rituals that structure most Heathen practice, the rites of passage that mark the significant transitions of a human life, and the small, daily gestures through which the tradition inhabits ordinary existence.

Sacred Space: Hof and Hörgr

Worship in Asatru takes place in two kinds of space, each serving a distinct purpose.

The hof is a communal hall—a roofed, dedicated space used by a kindred or group for regular ritual gatherings. In the Viking Age, the hof was a permanent structure, sometimes associated with a specific family or chieftain, where the seasonal blóts and communal ceremonies took place. In modern Asatru, a hof can be a dedicated building, a regularly used outdoor site, or simply the space within a home that a kindred has consecrated for group use. What makes a hof is not its architecture but its consistent dedication—the fact that it has been hallowed and is maintained as a place where the gods are regularly invited.

The hörgr is something more personal: an altar or shrine, often outdoors, traditionally built from piled or stacked stone. Where the hof is communal, the hörgr is the practitioner's private interface with the sacred—a physical focal point for individual practice, offerings, and communication with the gods, ancestors, and land spirits. In practice, a hörgr can be as simple as a shelf in a home set with significant objects, a stone cairn in the garden, or a dedicated corner of a room. The material matters less than the intention. What makes a hörgr is that it has been set apart—understood, by both practitioner and whatever forces are being honored there, as a threshold between the ordinary world and the sacred one.

Both spaces are consecrated before use, typically through the Hammer Hallowing—a ritual in which the officiant traces the shape of Mjölnir in the four cardinal directions while invoking Thor's protection, establishing the boundaries of sacred space and marking it as distinct from the everyday world surrounding it.

The Blót

The blót (pronounced roughly "bloat") is the central act of Asatru worship—the ritual offering through which practitioners establish and renew their relationship with the divine. The word's Old Norse root carries connotations of both sacrifice and hallowing, and both meanings are active in the ritual's structure.

In the pre-Christian Norse world, the blót typically involved an animal dedicated to a specific god and then sacrificed, with the blood used to consecrate the participants and the altar, and the meat shared in a communal feast. The offering was understood not as a transaction—paying the god for services rendered or hoped for—but as a gift: the Norse understanding of the gift relationship (gebo, as the rune has it) as the foundation of all meaningful bonds. You give to the god because you are in relationship with the god, and the gift renews and deepens that relationship.

Modern Asatru practice has largely adapted the blót away from animal sacrifice—partly for practical reasons, partly because the relationship between modern practitioners and livestock is so different from that of a farming culture that the original form would be more theatrical than meaningful. The standard modern blót uses mead, ale, or juice as the offering, maintaining the essential structure while adapting it honestly to contemporary life.

The blót follows a three-part structure. First, the hallowing: the space is consecrated, the deity being honored is invoked, and the offering is consecrated—typically by the goði or gyðja (priest or priestess) holding the horn aloft and tracing the Hammer sign over it while calling on the god to accept and bless what is given. The posture associated with invocation in most Heathen practice is the elhaz position—arms raised and open, fingers spread, mirroring the shape of the protection rune—an attitude of openness to divine contact rather than supplication before a superior power. Asatruar stand before their gods; they do not kneel.

Second, the sharing: the blessed horn is passed among those present, each drinking in turn. This moment is theologically significant. The mead, having been offered to and accepted by the deity, carries that divine presence when drunk. The communal drinking goes beyond symbolic fellowship—it is understood as a literal incorporation of the god's blessing into the body of each participant. The community becomes, through this act, a single body sharing a single gift.

Third, the libation: the remaining mead is poured into a hlautbolli (a con-secration bowl) and then given to the earth—poured out onto the ground as an offering to Jörð, the earth herself, completing the circuit of exchange between the human community, the divine, and the living world that sus-tains both. This final pouring is often accompanied by words of thanks and a traditional formula acknowledging both the deity honored and the earth that receives the gift.

A blót can be performed in five minutes alone at a home altar or as the cen-terpiece of a large communal gathering lasting several hours. What varies is the scale and elaboration—the essential structure remains the same. The parent who pours a quick offering of mead to Eir before sitting with a sick child is performing the same fundamental act as a kindred gathered for the winter solstice. The relationship being honored is what matters, not the ceremony surrounding it.

The Sumbel

If the blót is primarily directed outward—toward the gods, the land, the ancestors—the sumbel is primarily directed inward, toward the commu-nity itself. The word appears in Beowulf as one of the first acts Beowulf performs upon arriving at Hrothgar's hall: a formal drinking ceremony through which identity and intent are declared in a sacred context.

The sumbel is simpler in structure than the blót. Participants are seated in a circle or hall. A horn of mead is passed around the assembled group. Each per-son, when the horn reaches them, makes a toast—to the gods, to honored an-cestors or historical figures, to their own achievements or intentions—drinks, and passes the horn on. The critical feature of the sumbel is that words spoken over the horn are understood to carry special weight. The Norse tradition held that speech, particularly formal speech in a ritual context, was a form of ac-tion—that what you declared at sumbel entered the web of wyrd and became part of the pattern of what would unfold. A boast made at sumbel was not merely a statement of intention. It was a commitment, witnessed by the gods and the community, that shaped what you were now obligated to become.

Three-round formats are common. The first round honors the gods—toasts to specific deities, acknowledgments of their presence and power. The second honors the ancestors and heroes—historical figures, saga characters, the dead of one's own family line. The third is personal—a space for individual toasts, boasts of past achievements, or geas (pledges of future action). This third round carries the most weight and the most risk: what you say you will do, you have now said you will do, in front of the gods and your community.

The sumbel is also a space for storytelling, poetry, and song—for the recitation of verses from the Hávamál, for the sharing of saga episodes relevant to the occasion, for the performance of original compositions honoring the gods or the kindred's history. In this way, it functions as both a religious ceremony and a community-building practice, the formal context in which the bonds of a kindred are regularly renewed and deepened.

Profession

Profession is the ritual by which a person formally dedicates themselves to Asatru—the equivalent, in rough terms, of Christian confirmation or the Wiccan initiation. Unlike those analogues, it involves no transformation of status, no esoteric transmission, and no gatekeeping on the part of the officiating goði. It is precisely what its name suggests: a public declaration of intent.

The ritual is brief. In the presence of the community and before an altar, the person professing holds the oath ring—a sacred object on which binding commitments are made—and speaks their vow of loyalty and kinship to the gods and to the Heathen path. The specific words vary between kindreds and traditions, but the substance is consistent: I am here of my own will, I choose this path freely, I pledge my faithfulness to the Æsir and Vanir.

Two points about Profession deserve emphasis. First, it should not be undertaken lightly or under social pressure. A vow made at sumbel is binding; a vow made at Profession is made before the gods themselves. It should be the product of serious reflection and deliberate choice. Second—and this bears repeating—no one needs to have professed in order to participate in Asatru practice. The rituals, the seasonal gatherings, the blóts and sumbels, are open to anyone with sincere interest. Profession is for those who have found their home in the tradition and want to name that fact formally.

Rites of Passage

The major transitions of human life—birth, naming, coming of age, marriage, death—are marked in Asatru through rites that connect the individual moment to the larger pattern of the cosmos and the community.

Birth and Naming – The knésetja (knee-setting) is the traditional naming rite, in which the newborn is placed on the father's knee and formally given a name and family history at a community gathering. The name does more than identify—it connects the child to the ancestral line, to the hamingja (inherited luck) of those who came before, and to the pattern of fate that the Norns have already begun to weave. Many modern Heathen families maintain the tradition of offering nornagraut—a porridge made for the Norns as thanks for the child's safe arrival—and of marking the birth with a small communal gathering at which the child is welcomed into the kindred's circle.

Coming of Age – No pre-Christian rite of passage for adolescents has survived in the primary sources, which means modern Heathens have created their own. Common elements include the gifting of a first Mjölnir pendant, the presentation of a personal copy of the Eddas or the Hávamál, a formal acknowledgment by the community that the young person is entering adult responsibility, and—sometimes—a first participation in sumbel at which the young person makes their first formal toast. The specifics vary widely. What matters is the acknowledgment: this person is no longer a child. The community witnesses the transition and accepts the new set of expectations it implies.

Marriage – The Norse sources describe wedding ceremonies primarily through incidental references rather than systematic accounts. What is consistent is the role of Mjölnir: the hammer was placed in the bride's lap to consecrate the union—invoking Thor's blessing on the new household and on the fertility of the partnership. Modern Heathen weddings typically follow this structure, with the goði or gyðja officiating, oaths exchanged over the oath ring, and the hammer blessing given. In Scandinavia, the national Asatru organizations are legally authorized to officiate at civil weddings. In other countries, this varies by jurisdiction, but the ritual form is observed regardless of its legal status.

Death – The most extensively documented of the Norse rites of passage, the funeral involved the return of the dead to the elements—typically through cremation, sometimes burial—accompanied by grave goods, a final horn of mead poured as libation, and the formal recounting of the deceased's deeds and name. The erfiöl—the memorial ale drunk after the funeral—was both a farewell and an act of ancestor veneration: the dead person entered, through this rite, the community of honored ancestors who would henceforth be acknowledged at the seasonal gatherings. Modern Heathen funerals maintain these elements in adapted form. Cremation is common and consistent with the tradition. The recounting of the deceased's deeds—their dómr, their legacy—is understood as a final act of honor that names what they leave behind in the web of wyrd.

Daily Practice

The major rituals structure the year. Daily practice inhabits the ordinary hours.

The simplest and most widespread is the hammer sign—tracing the shape of Mjölnir over food, drink, or a threshold before use or passage, a gesture of blessing and acknowledgment that takes three seconds and can be performed anywhere without explanation. It is the most accessible entry point into embodied Heathen practice: a physical act that interrupts the automatic flow of daily life and inserts a moment of intention.

Many practitioners maintain a daily offering—a small cup of mead or ale, a piece of bread, a flower from the garden—left at the home altar for the land-vættir, the house spirits, or the gods currently being honored. The gesture is modest. The relationship it maintains is not.

Prayer—spoken aloud rather than silently, in the Norse tradition—is addressed directly to specific gods, in specific circumstances. Óðinn before any act requiring wisdom or creativity. Thor when strength or protection is needed. Freya at times of love, loss, or magical working. The gods are not addressed as distant abstractions but as senior members of an extended family: spoken to with respect, with honesty, and with the expectation that the relationship is real enough to bear the weight of direct communication.

Finally, the acknowledgment of place: arriving somewhere new, taking a moment to acknowledge the landvættir of that specific location. Leaving an offering before beginning work on a garden or a building project. Noticing the land beneath your feet as something inhabited, not just something owned. This is perhaps the quietest form of Heathen practice, and perhaps the most continuously demanding—the cultivation of an attention that recognizes the sacred in the ordinary without requiring a ceremony to do so.

Asatru is a religion of the threshold—the moment where one thing gives way to another, where the ordinary world and the sacred one touch. The rituals in this chapter mark the major thresholds: the turning of the year, the transitions of a life, the encounter with the divine in communal ceremony. Daily practice marks all the smaller ones. Together, they constitute a way of inhabiting the world that is, in the oldest sense of the word, religious: bound, attentive, and oriented toward something larger than the self.

Chapter 12

The Sacred Calendar of Asatru

Time, for the pre-Christian Norse, was not a neutral container in which events happened to occur. It was a living structure—cyclical, layered, and saturated with meaning. The year turned like a wheel, each season carrying its own character, its own demands, its own relationship to the divine forces that governed the world. The people who planted and harvested, who sailed and fought and wintered in darkness, understood their lives as embedded in that turning—not as observers of natural cycles but as participants in them.

Modern Asatru inherits this orientation. The eight holy tides of the Heathen calendar are not arbitrary commemorations. They mark the actual astronomical and agricultural rhythms of the Northern European year—the solstices and equinoxes, the midpoints between them—and connect the practitioner's daily life to the mythological events and divine forces most active at each turning. Observing the calendar is not an obligation imposed from outside. It is a practice of alignment: of bringing your attention, your offerings, and your community into relationship with the forces that are already moving through the world at that moment.

Not every kindred observes all eight holy tides with equal elaboration. What matters is the habit of acknowledgment—the practice of pausing at each turning of the year to mark what is shifting, to honor the relevant gods and ancestors, and to bring the invisible rhythms of the cosmos into the visible life of the community.

Yule

Jól — Sunset of the winter solstice through January 1st

Yule is the most important festival in the Heathen year—twelve days of celebration beginning at sunset on the winter solstice, the longest night, and extending through the new year. Its Old Norse name, Jól, derives from a word meaning "wheel," a direct reference to the sun as a wheel of fire rolling through the sky and reaching its lowest point before beginning its return. The darkness is at its deepest. The return of the light is imminent but not yet certain. The community gathers to witness the turning and to ensure, through ritual attention and celebration, that the sun finds its way back.

The first night of Yule—Modraniht, the Mother's Night—is dedicated to Frigg and the dísir, the female ancestral spirits. A vigil is kept from dark to dawn, welcoming the sun's return. This is a night for quiet reflection and ancestor acknowledgment, for setting intentions for the year ahead, and for the particular kind of attention that the long darkness makes possible.

The twelve days that follow are characterized by feasting, gift-giving, storytelling, and the swearing of sacred oaths. The oath-taking tradition—pledging commitments for the coming year over a holy horn at the Yule feast—is the ancient origin of the modern New Year's resolution, stripped of its sacred weight. In Asatru practice, the Yule oath is taken seriously: spoken before the gods and community, witnessed by both, binding in the way that all words spoken at a ritual gathering are binding.

Odin walks closest to Miðgarðr at Yule, moving through the world in the guise of the wandering Jólnir—the Yule One—from whom the figure of Santa Claus descends more directly than most people realize. The Wild Hunt rides. The dead move closer to the living. The Yule tree, the burning log, the decorated wreath, the gifts hung on branches—all of it traces directly to the Heathen celebration that Christian missionaries found impossible to suppress and instead absorbed, thinly reframed, into the new religion's calendar. Yule is a time for community, for honoring the ancestors alongside the living, for making the commitments that will define the year to come, and for the deep satisfaction of sitting in warmth and firelight while the darkness reaches its furthest extent outside—knowing that the wheel is already turning back.

Disting

Dísablót — January 31st

Disting is the quieter, more domestic counterpart to the grand celebration of Yule—a feast of new beginnings that looks forward rather than inward. Its name translates as "Thing of the Goddesses," and it was historically the first public festival of the year in Sweden, coinciding with the earliest preparations for the coming agricultural season.

The dísir—the female ancestral spirits—are the focus of this feast, honored for their ongoing protection of the family line and petitioned for their blessing on the work of the year ahead. Where Yule acknowledges the turning of the cosmic wheel, Disting turns the practitioner's attention to the practical: the fields that will need planting, the projects that will need beginning, the intentions set at Yule that now require the first acts of effort to make them real.

In modern practice, Disting is often a smaller, more intimate observance than the major holy tides—a home altar offering to the dísir, a blót of mead poured with thanks for the protection the ancestors have provided through the dark months, and a quiet acknowledgment that the light is returning and the work is beginning. It is a festival that rewards the practitioner who has been paying attention to the domestic rhythms of their life—who notices the first lengthening of the days, the first restlessness that follows the winter's rest—rather than one who requires elaborate ceremony to feel the sacred.

Ostara

Spring Equinox — March 21st

Ostara marks the spring equinox—the moment when day and night stand in exact balance before the light takes precedence. Named for the Germanic goddess of spring and the dawn, whose name shares its root with the words for "east" and "morning," this feast commemorates the earth's return to fertility, the cracking of winter's grip, and the beginning of the season of growth.

The goddess Ostara is among the more historically elusive figures in the Norse pantheon—her name and cult were recorded primarily by the Venerable Bede, and the primary sources are thin. What is beyond dispute is the antiquity of the celebration itself: spring equinox festivals are among the oldest recorded human observances, and the customs associated with Ostara—decorated eggs, the hare as sacred animal, bonfires lit at dawn to greet the sun—are documented in Germanic folk tradition stretching back well before the Viking Age. The Christian feast of Easter takes both its name and many of its symbols directly from this older celebration, a borrowing so complete that the original has become almost invisible beneath it.

In modern Asatru, Ostara is celebrated as the feast of the waking earth—a time for outdoor rituals that acknowledge the return of the land spirits after winter, for offerings of first flowers and seeds, and for the ritual planting of intentions that will be cultivated through the summer months. It is a natural complement to the inward focus of Yule and Disting: where those festivals honored darkness and ancestry, Ostara turns outward, toward growth, toward the warmth that is now definitively returning, toward the living world coming back into its power.

May Eve

Walpurgis — April 30th

May Eve falls at the midpoint between the spring equinox and the summer solstice—the moment when winter has definitively ended and summer's energy is beginning to build toward its peak. It is a festival of love, of magic, of the fertile forces that are now fully awake in the land, and of the threshold between the ordered world of settlement and the wild world of the forest and the open country beyond it.

Freya presides over May Eve in her dual aspect—as goddess of love and desire, and as mistress of seiðr, the most potent magical practice in the Norse tradition. Both aspects are appropriate to a night that has been understood, across Germanic cultures for centuries, as a time when the boundary between the ordinary world and the world of magical forces becomes unusually permeable. Bonfires lit on hilltops at dusk mark the transition, their light simultaneously celebrating the return of warmth and serving as a protective boundary against the more chaotic forces that move freely on this night.

The maypole—danced around in Scandinavian and Germanic folk tradition on this night and the following day—is among the most ancient fertility symbols in Northern European practice, its raising a ritual enactment of the union of earth and sky, of the generative principle made physically present in the community's gathering place. The flowers and greenery woven into its decorations are offerings to the land spirits and to Freya herself, acknowledgments that the fertility of the coming growing season is not automatic but relational—the result of a living exchange between the human community and the forces that govern growth.

May Eve is one of the most celebratory holy tides—a time for outdoor gathering, for bonfires, for honoring Freya and Freyr in their aspects of love and fertility, and for the kind of joyful, communal energy that the long northern winter makes precious. It is also a time for seiðr work and magical practice, the veil between worlds being understood as thinner than usual, and the powers invoked in magical working as correspondingly more accessible.

Midsummer

Summer Solstice — June 21st

Midsummer is the year's peak—the longest day, the point at which the sun's power reaches its absolute maximum before beginning its slow descent toward winter. It is simultaneously a celebration of abundance fully realized and an acknowledgment that the wheel has turned to its highest point and will now, inevitably, begin to turn back. Both truths belong to the festival, and the best Midsummer observances hold both without collapsing one into the other.

Baldr is the mythological figure most associated with Midsummer—the radiant god of light and purity whose death, caused by Loki's manipulation of Höðr and the mistletoe dart, marks the moment when the year's light begins to diminish. In the mythological calendar, his death falls at the solstice: the sun is at its brightest, and it is precisely at that brightness that the shadow falls. Offerings to Baldr at Midsummer acknowledge both his beauty and the inevitability of what follows—understanding his story as a mythological encoding of the year's most fundamental rhythm.

The traditional celebrations of Midsummer are among the most elaborate and widespread in the Germanic world: massive bonfires built on hilltops or cliff edges, visible across the countryside; wreath-making from midsummer flowers; the decoration of boats with greenery and the setting of small votive ships alight on the water; feasting that extends through the brief northern night. In Scandinavia, Midsummer remains the most widely observed folk festival of the year, celebrated by Heathens and non-Heathens alike with a continuity of custom that has survived a thousand years of Christianity without serious disruption.

Midsummer calls for outdoor community gathering on the largest scale the kindred can manage—honoring the gods in their summer aspects: Thor as protector of the fields and the people who depend on them, Freyr as the god of summer fertility, Baldr as the emblem of the light that must eventually be lost.

It is a time for courage and action—the Viking sailing season began after Midsummer, when the crops were safely planted and the summer's abundance was assured—and for the particular quality of gratitude that comes from standing in the full warmth of a long northern day and knowing, with complete clarity, that this is as good as it gets.

Freyfest

Lammas — July 31st

Freyfest falls at the midpoint between the summer solstice and the autumn equinox—the festival of first harvest, when the earliest crops begin to come in and the long season of growth and tending begins to yield its results. Its English name, Lammas, derives from the Anglo-Saxon hlaf-maesse, "loaf-feast," a direct reference to the bread baked from the first grain of the harvest and offered in thanks for what the earth has produced.

Freyr is the presiding deity—god of the sun's warmth, the rain's blessing, and the earth's fertility, whose entire mythological character is oriented toward abundance, peace, and the pleasures of a good harvest. His sacred animal, the boar, is honored at this feast; his association with bread and grain makes Freyfest the most naturally agricultural of the holy tides, the one most directly connected to the experience of a farming people watching the year's labor begin to manifest in tangible form.

Thor is also honored at Freyfest, particularly in his role as the god of the common people—the protector of farmers and ordinary households, the one whose hammer blesses hearth and field as readily as it defends against giants. His wife Sif, whose long golden hair the tradition connects to the rippling fields of ripe wheat, receives acknowledgment alongside him. The images are satisfyingly concrete: the golden grain standing in the fields, the first loaves cooling on the hearth, the community gathering to acknowledge that the work of spring and summer has not been in vain.

In modern Asatru practice, Freyfest is celebrated with offerings of bread and grain, with the baking of traditional loaves shared communally and offered to the gods, and with the particular gratitude that attends the first visible results of months of effort. It is a feast that rewards practicality and patience—the qualities that got the seed into the ground and tended it through the growing months—and connects those mundane virtues to the sacred exchange between the human community and the divine forces that govern fertility.

Fallfest

Haustblót — September 23rd

Fallfest marks the autumn equinox—the second moment in the year when day and night stand in exact balance, this time with darkness gaining the upper hand. Where Ostara celebrated the balance tipping toward light, Fallfest acknowledges the tipping toward dark. The harvest is at its fullest, the storehouses filling, the work of the growing season reaching its conclusion. It is a feast of completion and of gratitude, but also of sober acknowledgment: winter is coming, and what has been gathered must sustain the community through the months ahead.

The agricultural significance of this feast is immediate and concrete. For a farming people, the autumn equinox marked the point at which the year's success or failure could finally be assessed. The animals that would not survive the winter were slaughtered, their meat preserved for the cold months. The last of the harvest was brought in. The community took stock of what it had. In many Germanic traditions, communal bonfires were lit at Fallfest, their flames drawn from a central fire from which each family then relit their own hearth—a ritual enactment of the community's shared dependence and shared survival, the dispersal of a single sacred flame into every household simultaneously.

The gods honored at Fallfest are those of abundance and protection: Freyr and Freya for the harvest's fertility, Thor for the protection of the household through the coming winter, the ancestors for the accumulated wisdom of previous winters survived. Offerings reflect the season—grain, vegetables, the first of the preserved meats, apples, and the rich amber mead traditionally brewed from the honey harvested in late summer.

Fallfest is a time for honest assessment alongside gratitude—for examining what the year has actually produced, what intentions set at Yule and Ostara have borne fruit and which have not, and for approaching the turn toward darkness with the clear-eyed equanimity that the Norse tradition has always valued more than false optimism. The wheel is turning toward winter. The light is diminishing. The community has what it has gathered. This is sufficient, and it is cause for celebration.

Winter Nights

Vetrnætr — October 31st

Winter Nights is the last and in many ways the most spiritually significant of the eight holy tides—the feast that closes the cycle of the year, bridges the gap between summer and winter, and opens the time when the worlds draw closest together. Its name in Old Norse, Vetrnætr, means simply "Winter Nights," and it marks the ancient Norse new year: the beginning of the winter half of the year, when the attention of the community turns from the external work of farming and sailing to the internal work of memory, craft, and community.

The boundary between the living and the dead is at its thinnest on this night. The Wild Hunt begins its ride. The draugr stir. The ancestors return to the warmth of the fires they once kept. In the old tradition, food and drink were set out for the returning dead, and the feast that followed was shared, in imagination if not in physical presence, with all the generations that had preceded the living community. This is not metaphor. It is a theological statement about the ongoing relationship between the living and the dead that sits at the heart of Heathen practice—the understanding that the community extends backward in time as far as memory reaches and forward as far as the lineage continues.

The dísir, the female ancestral spirits, are particularly active at Winter Nights, and a dísablót—an offering to the ancestral women of the family line—is traditionally performed by the woman of the household, the ritual role of dísablót being one of the few explicitly female priestly functions in the Norse tradition. Freyr and Freya are also honored, in their aspects as gods of abundance and of the passage between life and death.

Winter Nights is the most important ancestor feast of the year—a time for setting out offerings at the home altar for those who have died, for speaking the names of the ancestors aloud, for telling their stories to those who did not know them, and for the particular quality of presence that comes from acknowledging yourself as a link in a chain that extends far beyond your individual life. The Christian calendar absorbed this feast as Halloween and All Saints' Day, retaining its focus on the dead while stripping it of the reciprocal, relational understanding that gave it meaning. Modern Heathens reclaim that original depth.

Lesser Feasts: Days of Remembrance

In addition to the eight holy tides, the modern Heathen calendar includes a series of Days of Remembrance—commemorations of historical figures from the Norse and Germanic traditions who embodied Heathen values and whose stories are worth keeping alive. These are smaller observances, typically marked with a brief blót and a toast at sumbel rather than a full community gathering.

January 9th — Raud the Strong, a Norwegian chieftain who died rather than convert to Christianity under Olaf Tryggvason.

February 9th — Eyvind Kinnrif, who likewise died under torture rather than renounce the old gods.

February 14th — Feast of Vali, honoring the god of vengeance and the return of light in the depths of winter.

March 28th — Ragnar Lodbrok, the celebrated Viking chieftain whose life and death exemplify the warrior's code.

April 9th — Hákon Sigurdsson, a defender of Heathenry in Norway during the forced Christian conversions.

May 9th — Gudrod of Gudbrandsdal, a martyr of the old faith who refused Christian rule.

June 9th — Sigurd the Dragon-slayer, the great hero of the Völsunga Saga.

July 9th — Unn the Deep-Minded, one of the most important leaders of the Icelandic settlement.

August 9th — King Radbod of Frisia, who at the moment of his baptism asked whether he would meet his pagan ancestors in heaven or in hell—and upon learning he would be separated from them forever, withdrew his foot from the font and died a Heathen.

September 9th — Hermann the Cheruscan, who preserved Germanic culture and language by defeating the Roman legions in the Teutoburg Forest.

October 9th — Leif Eriksson's Day, honoring the Norse explorer and his sister Freydis Eriksdottir, who led the first known European settlement in North America.

October 28th — Erik the Red, founder of the first settlement in Greenland.

November 9th — Queen Sigrid of Sweden, who refused to abandon the gods of her fathers and helped bring about the downfall of Olaf Tryggvason.

November 11th — Feast of the Einherjar, honoring all those who died with honor and now dwell in Valhalla and the halls of the gods.

November 27th — Feast of Ullr and Skadi, and of Weyland the Smith—a day honoring the great craftspeople of the Germanic tradition.

December 9th — Egill Skallagrímsson, poet, warrior, and rune-master of the Viking Age.

These Days of Remembrance serve a specific function in Heathen practice: they keep the tradition's human history alive, connecting modern practitioners to the chain of people who lived and died by these values across the centuries. The gods are eternal. The ancestors are finite. Both deserve acknowledgment, and the Days of Remembrance ensure that the finite ones are not forgotten.

What the Calendar Is For

The eight holy tides and the Days of Remembrance together constitute a complete framework for inhabiting time as a Heathen—for experiencing the year not as a neutral sequence of months but as a living structure with its own rhythms, its own demands, and its own gifts.

The practitioner who observes the calendar seriously will find that it gradually reshapes their relationship to time itself. The solstices and equinoxes become events felt in the body rather than astronomical abstractions. The ancestors become present at Winter Nights in a way that grows more real with each year of practice. The gods associated with each season become more vivid as their festivals approach and recede. The wheel turns, and the practitioner turns with it—oriented, rooted, and aware of their place in a pattern that extends far beyond the boundaries of a single human life.

That awareness is, in the end, what the calendar is for.

Chapter 13

Death, the Afterlife, and Ancestors

T here is a question that every serious spiritual tradition must eventually answer, and the Norse tradition answers it with unusual directness: what happens when we die?

The directness is not comforting in the way that many modern people hope a religious answer will be comforting. There is no universal salvation, no guaranteed reunion with the beloved dead, no single destination that awaits all souls regardless of how they lived. What the Norse tradition offers instead is something more complex and, in its way, more honest: a differentiated understanding of death as a transition rather than an ending, a cosmos in which the dead continue to exist in various forms and various relationships with the living, and a set of practices for maintaining those relationships across the boundary that death creates.

Death, in this tradition, is not the enemy of a life well lived. It is its completion—the point at which the sum of a person's deeds, the quality of their relationships, and the strength of the hamingja they leave behind become fixed in the web of wyrd, permanent and unalterable. The Norse were not afraid of death. They were concerned with dying well—with meeting the end of life in a way that honored what had come before and left something worth inheriting behind.

This chapter explores what the tradition actually believes about what follows death, what aspects of the self survive and in what form, and how modern Asatruar maintain living relationships with those who have gone before them.

Death as Transition

The Norse understanding of death was shaped by a cosmological framework that had no room for the sharp binary of heaven and hell that Christianity later imposed on Northern Europe. The dead did not go to one place. They went to many places, depending on how they had lived, how they had died, and what arrangements the living made for their passage.

This plurality reflects something important about the Norse worldview: the refusal to reduce complex realities to simple categories. Life was varied and multidimensional. Death, in this framework, was equally so. The warrior who fell in battle occupied a different position in the cosmos than the farmer who died of old age in his bed, who occupied a different position than the oath-breaker whose restless spirit could not settle, who occupied a different position than the revered ancestor whose hamingja continued to bless the family line generations after the body had returned to earth.

What this means practically is that the Norse approach to death was not primarily about destination—about where you end up—but about the quality of the transition and the ongoing relationship between the living and the dead. The funeral rites were not simply disposal of the body. They were the first acts of a continuing relationship, designed to ensure that the dead were properly honored, properly sent, and properly positioned to continue contributing to the welfare of those they had left behind.

The Hávamál states it plainly: cattle die, kinsmen die, the self must also die. What does not die is the reputation—the dómr—that a person leaves behind. This is not a metaphor for being remembered fondly. It is a theological claim about the structure of reality: that the deeds of a life become, at death, a permanent feature of the web of wyrd, influencing the possibilities available to those who come after just as surely as any physical inheritance.

The Destinations of the Dead

The Norse afterlife was not a single place but a collection of distinct destinations, each suited to different kinds of death and different qualities of life.

Valhalla is the most famous—the great hall of Óðinn in Ásgarðr where the Einherjar, the chosen slain, feast and fight in preparation for Ragnarök. Entry to Valhalla required dying in battle and being selected by the Valkyries, Óðinn's choosers of the slain. It was not a reward for virtue in the general sense but a specific conscription: Óðinn needed warriors, and the best warriors were taken. Only a fraction of those who died in battle were selected; the rest went elsewhere. Valhalla was not the Norse heaven. It was Óðinn's army.

Fólkvangr—Freya's field—received the other half of those who fell in battle. Less is said about it in the primary sources than about Valhalla, which has led to it being overshadowed in popular consciousness. What is clear is that Freya's selection was no less real or honorable than Óðinn's—and given Freya's complexity as a goddess of both love and war, her domain may have been understood as offering a different quality of afterlife rather than a lesser one.

Fólkvangr deserves more attention than the primary sources give it—and more than it typically receives in modern treatments of the Norse afterlife. The asymmetry in the surviving accounts almost certainly reflects the biases of the medieval scholars who recorded them, most of whom were more interested in Óðinn's martial preparations for Ragnarök than in Freya's domain. What we can reconstruct suggests something worth taking seriously. Freya is the tradition's most powerful practitioner of seiðr, a goddess who moves between love and death with equal authority, who weeps tears of gold for an absent husband and claims half the battle-slain without contradiction. A realm presided over by her would not be a consolation prize. It would reflect her nature—wilder, less hierarchical than Valhalla, oriented toward the forces of fertility and magic rather than military discipline. Some modern practitioners understand Fólk-vangr as the destination for those whose relationship with Freya was close during life, or whose deaths carried the quality of sacrifice rather than pure martial valor. The sources do not confirm this, but neither do they contradict it. What they make clear is that Freya's choice was sovereign and deliberate—she took her half, and her half was equal.

Helheim received the majority of the dead: those who died of age, illness, acci-dent, the ordinary causes that take most lives. Governed by Hel—daughter of Loki, calm and consistent in her administration of the realm beneath Yggdrasil's deepest root—it was a place of rest and continuation rather than punishment. The Christian associations of the name "Hell" with torment and fire have noth-ing to do with the Norse Helheim, which was described as shadowed and still but not cruel. Most people went there. It was not a failure.

The burial mound represents a fourth possibility that sits outside the tripartite structure of Valhalla, Fólkvangr, and Helheim—and in many ways it may have been the most practically significant in the daily life of Norse communities. The dead were understood to remain in some meaningful sense within or near their burial place, connected to the land they had worked and the family they had loved. Ancestors honored with proper burial and regular offerings continued to bless the land above them and the people who tended it. This was not metaphor. The Norse genuinely understood the dead as present, local, and responsive to attention.

Reincarnation within the family line appears in several saga accounts, typi-cally associated with the transmission of hamingja—the inherited luck that passes from ancestor to descendant. A child born shortly after the death of a family elder might be named for that elder, understood as carrying forward some essential quality of the deceased. The boundaries between this belief and the ancestor-veneration practices centered on burial mounds were fluid; both reflected the understanding that death was a change of form rather than an absolute ending.

The Multiple Soul: What Survives

One of the most distinctive features of the Norse understanding of death is its conception of the human self as multiple rather than singular. Where the Christian tradition developed the idea of a single, indivisible soul that departs the body at death, the Norse tradition understood the self as composed of several semi-independent aspects, each with its own fate at death.

Chapter 1 introduced these briefly. Here they deserve fuller treatment, because understanding what the Norse believed about the structure of the self is inseparable from understanding what they believed about death.

The hamr—the shape, the appearance, the outer form through which a person presents themselves to the world—does not survive death. It is left behind with the body, returning to the earth from which it came. Skilled practitioners of seiðr could alter their hamr during life, projecting it at a distance or assuming the shape of animals. At death, that capacity ends.

The hugr—the mind, the will, the seat of conscious agency—also departs at death, though its ultimate fate varies by account. Some sources suggest it dissipates; others hint at a more complex continuation. What is consistent is that the hugr is understood as the most individual and most mortal aspect of the self—the part most tied to the specific personality of the living person.

The fylgja—the follower, the fetch—is the semi-autonomous spiritual companion that accompanies a person through life and is sometimes visible to those with the ability to perceive it, often in animal form. The fylgja is connected to fate and to the deeper pattern of a person's life in ways that transcend ordinary consciousness. At death, the fylgja may pass to a descendant, continuing its role of companionship and guidance in the next generation of the family line.

The hamingja—the luck, the accumulated spiritual force generated by honorable living—is the aspect of the self most explicitly understood as transmissible across generations. A person of strong hamingja leaves a legacy that actively improves the fortune of their descendants. A person who lived dishonorably, who broke oaths and accumulated níð (dishonor), leaves a diminished or con-taminated inheritance that their descendants must work to redeem. The ham-ingja is not merely a metaphor for influence or example. It is understood as a real spiritual substance, as tangible in its effects as any physical inheritance.

This multi-part understanding of the self means that death is not a single event but a process of dissolution and redistribution—different aspects of the person going different directions, some dissipating, some transmitting, some remaining in some form connected to the places and people the living person loved. The ancestor who is present at Winter Nights, who blesses the land they once farmed, who passes their luck forward through the bloodline—this is not sentimentality. It is a description, in mythological terms, of how the Norse believed the structure of the cosmos actually worked.

The Living Practice of Ancestor Veneration

The relationship between the living and the dead in Asatru is not one of mourn-ing and release—the modern Western model in which grief is a process to be completed, the dead gradually receding from active significance as the living move forward. It is a relationship of ongoing reciprocity, maintained through deliberate practice, that benefits both parties.

The ancestors need acknowledgment. Without it, their memory fades, their names are lost, and the connection between the living family and the accu-mulated hamingja of the lineage weakens. In extreme cases—when the dead are neglected, when proper burial was not given, when the relationship was severed by dishonor—the result was the draugr: the restless dead returning not in peace but in destruction, the dark consequence of a broken relationship that the tradition described in mythological terms but understood as a real spiritual danger.

The living need the ancestors. The hamingja that flows through a family line is not generated by the living alone—it is accumulated over generations, each honorable life adding to a fund of luck and spiritual strength that belongs to the lineage rather than the individual. To neglect the ancestors is to cut yourself off from that source, to attempt to build a life without the foundation that those who came before you laid.

The practice of ancestor veneration in modern Asatru takes several forms, varying in elaboration from the simple to the ceremonially complex.

The most basic is naming: speaking the names of the dead aloud, regularly, in ritual contexts and in ordinary life. At sumbel, the second round of toasts traditionally honors the ancestors—historical figures as well as the practitioner's own dead. At seasonal gatherings, particularly at Winter Nights and Yule, the names of those who have died within the past year or within living memory are spoken over the feast. The act of naming is not nostalgic. It is an assertion that the named person continues to exist in a form that makes acknowledgment meaningful.

The ancestor altar is a physical focal point for this relationship—a dedicated space within the home where photographs, objects belonging to the dead, small offerings of food and drink, and written or spoken words can be directed toward those who have gone before. The altar is not a shrine in the sense of a place of worship. It is more like a seat kept at the table for someone who has stepped temporarily out of the room—an acknowledgment that the absent one still belongs here, still participates in the life of the household, still receives consideration in decisions that affect the family.

Offerings are the material expression of the relationship's continuity. Mead or ale poured at the base of a burial marker. A plate of food set out at Winter Nights for the returning dead. A small portion of a significant meal—a birthday feast, a wedding dinner—given to the ancestors alongside the living. The logic is the gift relationship that runs through all of Asatru's relationships with the sacred: you give, they give back, the bond is maintained. The specific offering matters less than the intention—the honest acknowledgment that the dead are being remembered, that their contribution to the living is recognized and honored.

Sitting out—útiseta—is the more intensive practice of going to a significant ancestral location, particularly a burial place, and remaining there in meditation or light trance, open to whatever communication or impression comes. The primary sources describe this as a real technique for receiving guidance from ancestors, and while modern practitioners approach it with varying degrees of literalism, the core practice—deliberate, physically located attention to ancestral presence—remains active in contemporary Heathenry — though what it actually involves is less dramatic than it might sound, and more demanding than it might appear.

The practitioner goes to a place with ancestral significance—a grave site, a location associated with a family member's life, or simply a piece of land that has been in the family for generations—and sits. Not meditating in any structured sense, not attempting to induce a vision, but simply remaining present and open for an extended period, typically at least an hour, often at dusk or in the hours before dawn when the boundary between states of awareness is naturally thinner. They bring an offering—mead, food, something that belonged to the person they are seeking contact with—and they speak the ancestor's name aloud. Then they wait, and they pay attention to what arises: a memory that surfaces unbidden, a shift in the quality of the air, a dream that comes that night, an unexpected clarity about a decision they have been avoiding. The tradition does not promise dramatic results. What it offers is the discipline of deliberate attention directed at a relationship that most modern people allow to dissolve by default. Whether what arises is understood as literal contact with the dead or as something more psychological is, in the end, a question each practitioner must answer for themselves. The practice itself does not require a settled answer to be worth doing.

The ancestors honored in these practices are not limited to blood relatives, though blood lineage carries particular weight in the tradition. They include the broader community of those who lived by the same values, who practiced the same faith, who built the tradition that the living are now carrying forward. The historical figures honored in the Days of Remembrance—Raud the Strong, Egill Skallagrímsson, Leif Eriksson—are ancestors in this extended sense: people whose deeds shaped the world in which modern Asatruar practice their faith, whose names deserve to be kept alive.

Death and the Heathen Life

What the Norse tradition's understanding of death ultimately offers is not comfort of the consoling kind but something arguably more valuable: a framework for living in full awareness of mortality without being paralyzed by it.

The knowledge that death is coming—that it comes for everyone, that the gods themselves will fall at Ragnarök—did not produce despair in the Norse worldview. It produced urgency. If the only thing that survives death in any permanent form is the reputation, the dómr, then how you live matters with unusual intensity. Every act of courage or cowardice, every oath kept or broken, every gesture of hospitality or its refusal, contributes to the pattern of a life that will, at death, become fixed. You cannot revise it afterward. You can only add to it now.

This is why the Heathen tradition places such weight on deeds rather than beliefs. What you profess to believe about the gods can change from moment to moment; what you actually do in the world accumulates into something permanent. The person of strong hamingja is not necessarily the person with the most refined theology. They are the person who showed up—who fulfilled their obligations, honored their relationships, contributed to their community, met difficulty with courage, and left behind something worth inheriting.

The Norse attitude toward grief follows from this framework. Grief is real and the tradition does not minimize it—the mourning of the gods for Baldr is one of the most powerful images in the entire mythology, every living thing weeping for the loss of the most beloved among them. But grief in the Norse tradition is not the final word. The dead are not simply gone. They are present in a different form, in a different relationship, accessible through the practices that maintain the connection. The loss is real; the relationship continues.

Those who lose someone close often find that the tradition's ancestor practices—the altar, the offerings, the naming at sumbel, the Winter Nights feast—provide a framework for grief that does not require the bereaved to choose between their pain and their faith. The pain is part of the practice. The ongoing relationship with the dead is part of the practice. Both are held within the same cosmological understanding, and the result is a way of grieving that is, paradoxically, less isolating than many modern secular approaches precisely because it insists that the dead are still present, still part of the community, still deserving of acknowledgment.

Death, in this tradition, asks something of the living: that they remember, that they honor, that they carry forward the hamingja that was entrusted to them by those who came before. It is a serious responsibility. It is also, once the practice is established, a source of real comfort—the comfort that comes not from being told that everything will be fine but from knowing that you are not alone, that the chain extends backward farther than you can see, and that every person who has ever lived well in this tradition has added something to the fund of strength and luck that you now carry.

The ancestors are present. Speak their names. Make the offering. Keep the connection alive.

Death is the chapter that all chapters of a human life eventually reach. The tradition this book has traced—its cosmology, its texts, its gods, its values, its magic, its symbols, its rituals—exists, in part, to prepare its practitioners for that chapter, to give it meaning, and to ensure that what a person has built during their lifetime continues to matter after they are gone.

The final chapter turns to the beginning: to the practical question of how someone who has read this far actually starts.

Chapter 14

How to Begin: Your First Steps

There is a moment that many people reach after a long encounter with Asatru—after reading the myths, sitting with the cosmology, feeling something real resonate in the values and the ritual framework—when the natural next question is simply: now what?

The question is a good one, and it deserves a direct answer. Asatru is a practice-based tradition. The understanding you have built through the previous chapters matters, but it becomes meaningful only when it finds expression in what you actually do—in the small daily gestures, the seasonal observances, the relationships with the gods and ancestors that deepen through consistent attention over time. Reading about the blót is not the same as making one. Knowing the names of the runes is not the same as working with them. The tradition lives in practice, and practice begins with a first step.

This chapter is about taking it.

Begin Where You Are

The most common mistake beginners make is waiting until they feel ready—until they know enough, until they have the right objects, until they find the right community, until something external grants them permission to begin. That permission will not come from outside. Asatru has no central authority, no ordaining body, no formal gatekeeping between the seeker and the practice.

You begin where you are, with what you have, in the time you have available.

If you have five minutes in the morning, that is enough to stand before an open window, speak the name of one god, and make a small acknowledgment of the day beginning. If you have a shelf, that is enough to start an altar. If you have a jar of honey and some water, that is enough to make a first offering. The elaboration comes later, as practice deepens and the relationship with the tradition becomes more established. What cannot be deferred is the beginning itself.

Start small and start honestly. The gods of Asatru have no patience for performance—for elaborate ceremonies conducted by someone who does not yet know why they are performing them. What they respond to, according to every practitioner who has worked seriously in this tradition, is sincere intention: the honest acknowledgment of their presence, the real commitment to showing up consistently rather than impressively.

Your First Altar

An altar—a hörgr in its simplest modern form—is the physical foundation of a home practice. It does not need to be large, elaborate, or expensive. It needs to be dedicated: set apart from the ordinary objects of daily life, maintained with regularity, and understood as a threshold space where the ordinary world and the sacred one touch.

A shelf, a windowsill, a small table, a flat stone in the garden—any of these will serve. What you place on it should reflect the specific relationships you are beginning to build. A representation of the deity you feel most drawn to: a small figure, an image, a symbol carved or drawn. A horn or a cup for offerings.

A candle. Perhaps a Mjölnir pendant, or a rune carved into wood, or an object that belonged to someone you are beginning to honor as an ancestor.

The altar is not decorative. It is functional—a place where offerings are made, where names are spoken, where the daily practice of acknowledgment takes physical form. Tend it regularly. Keep it clean. Replace offerings before they spoil. The quality of your attention to the altar reflects the quality of your attention to the relationships it represents.

Begin with one deity. The temptation, especially after reading a full survey of the Norse pantheon, is to honor all of them simultaneously—to place something for Óðinn and something for Thor and something for Freya and something for the ancestors all on the same shelf. Resist this. One deity, approached seriously and consistently, will teach you more in three months than a scattered acknowledgment of fifteen will teach you in a year. Choose the one whose domain most clearly maps onto your current life—your work, your struggles, your actual questions—and begin there.

Daily Practice

A daily practice does not require a ceremony. It requires a habit—a regular, consistent gesture of acknowledgment that over time becomes as natural as any other part of the day's rhythm.

The simplest daily practice is the morning acknowledgment: standing at your altar, speaking the name of the deity you are currently working with, making a small offering—a few drops of water, a piece of bread, a flower from the garden—and saying something. Not a formula. Something direct: a statement of what you are facing that day, a question you are carrying, a simple acknowledgment of presence. Speak aloud. The Norse tradition was an oral one, and the spoken word carries weight that silent thought does not.

The evening counterpart is the accounting: a brief reflection on whether your actions during the day have been consistent with the values you are working to embody. Not a judgment—Asatru does not traffic in guilt—but an honest assessment. Did you act with courage where courage was required? Were you honest when honesty was costly? Did you fulfill the obligations you had taken on? This kind of daily self-examination is among the most powerful practices the tradition supports, and it costs nothing but a few minutes of serious attention.

Make the hammer sign before meals. Acknowledge the land spirits when you arrive somewhere new. Speak the name of an ancestor at moments of difficulty, asking for the hamingja they have left you. These small gestures, repeated consistently, gradually reshape the texture of ordinary experience—not by making everything dramatic or sacred in an overwhelming sense, but by introducing a quality of attention to the ordinary that the tradition understands as itself a form of worship.

Reading the Lore

The primary sources—the Poetic Edda, the Prose Edda, the major sagas—are not optional background reading. They are the living foundation of the tradition, and a practitioner who does not engage with them directly is working at second hand, dependent on other people's interpretations rather than their own encounter with the material.

Begin with the Hávamál. Read it slowly, a few stanzas at a time, with a good translation and commentary alongside. Do not try to absorb it all at once. Live with individual verses for days or weeks before moving on. The Hávamál is practical wisdom, not mythology—it addresses directly how to live, how to think about relationships, how to navigate difficulty with honor—and it rewards the reader who brings their own current experience to the text rather than approaching it as historical literature to be understood at a distance.

From there, move to the Völuspá—the seeress's vision of the cosmos from creation to Ragnarök—and then to the prose narratives of the Prose Edda. The sagas can be approached in parallel, beginning with the Íslendingasögur that are most accessible to modern readers: Egils saga, Njáls saga, Laxdæla saga.

Return to the primary sources repeatedly as your practice develops. You will find different things in them at different points in your life, because what you bring to the texts changes as the practice deepens. A verse of the Hávamál that meant one thing at the beginning of your Heathen path will mean something richer and more specific after years of working with the tradition it describes.

Finding Community

Asatru can be practiced alone, and many people do so for months or years before finding a community that feels right. Solitary practice is legitimate and can be deeply meaningful—the relationship with the gods and ancestors does not require a kindred to be real.

But the tradition is fundamentally communal. The blót is most fully itself when shared. The sumbel requires others across the horn. The kindred—the community of practitioners who know each other, support each other, and hold each other accountable to the values they share—is the basic social unit of Heathen life, and a practitioner who remains isolated from community indefinitely misses something that solitary practice cannot provide.

Finding a kindred requires some effort, particularly outside of Scandinavia and North America where Heathen communities are most established. The Troth, the Asatru Folk Assembly, and the Asatru Alliance are among the larger American organizations, each with a directory of affiliated kindreds. In Europe, national organizations exist in Iceland, Denmark, Norway, Sweden, Germany, and the United Kingdom. Online communities—forums, social media groups, Discord servers—can provide connection and orientation while a practitioner is looking for local community, but they are better understood as supplements to in-person practice than substitutes for it.

When you do find a potential kindred, attend a few gatherings before making any commitment. The values of Asatru—honesty, honor, hospitality—should be visible in how the group actually operates, not just in what it claims to stand for. A kindred whose members treat each other with real respect and hold each other to real standards is worth traveling for. One whose practice is primarily social and whose values are primarily theoretical will not deepen your practice.

Pay attention, also, to the question of inclusivity. The Heathen community has not been immune to the contamination of racist ideology—a strand of so-called "folkish" Heathenry that restricts membership and practice by ethnic background has existed since the early revival. This position has no grounding in the actual historical practice of Norse religion, which was geographically expansive, ethnically diverse, and defined by cultural participation rather than bloodline. Any group that restricts membership or practice on racial grounds is practicing something other than authentic Asatru, and is best avoided.

On Patience and Expectation

The relationship with the gods in Asatru deepens slowly, and the early stages of practice are often characterized more by a quality of quiet attention than by dramatic spiritual experience. This is normal and should not be interpreted as failure.

The Norse gods are not in the business of overwhelming beginners with visions and signs. They respond to consistency, to earnest effort, to the practitioner who shows up with real intent rather than a desire for extraordinary experience. The sign that a practice is working is rarely a dramatic encounter with the divine—it is more often a gradual shift in how you inhabit your own life: a greater clarity about your values, a stronger capacity for honest self-assessment, a deepening sense of being part of something that extends beyond the boundaries of your individual existence.

Trust the slow accumulation. Make the offering. Speak the name. Read the lore. Return to practice after you have failed at it, without excessive drama in either direction. The tradition does not reward intensity of feeling. It rewards the consistent, honest effort that the Hávamál describes in a hundred different ways as the foundation of a life worth living.

A Last Word

Asatru does not ask you to believe anything you cannot verify. It asks you to practice—to show up, to make the offering, to speak the names, to observe the seasons, to live by the values, to maintain the relationships that the tradition identifies as sacred. Everything else follows from that.

The gods and ancestors of the Norse tradition have survived a thousand years of suppression, misrepresentation, and neglect. They are still here—present in the primary texts, alive in the practices of the communities that have maintained and reconstructed them, accessible to anyone who approaches them with honest intent and real respect.

The wheel is turning. The tree is standing. The runes are waiting in the well at the base of the roots.

Begin.

Conclusion

T here is a verse in the *Hávamál* that has stayed with practitioners of Asatru across generations of the modern revival, not because it is the most dramatic or the most quoted, but because it captures something essential about what this tradition actually asks of the people who enter it:

"Better to live, even to live miserably—a living man can always get a cow. I saw fire burning in a rich man's hall, but death stood at the door."

The Norse tradition is not a tradition of transcendence. It does not promise escape from the world as it actually is—from difficulty, from loss, from the knowledge that the roots of the tree are being gnawed even as the branches shelter the living. What it offers instead is something rarer and more demanding: a framework for living fully within that world, with clear eyes and genuine commitments, in relationship with forces larger than the individual self.

This is why Asatru continues to grow in a world that has no shortage of spiritual options. It is not growing because of aesthetics, though the mythology is extraordinary. It is not growing because of nostalgia, though the connection to ancestral tradition matters to many who find it. It is growing because something in the modern world has created a hunger for exactly what Asatru provides: a faith that does not ask you to believe the unbelievable, that locates the sacred in practice rather than in doctrine, that insists on personal responsibility rather than offering salvation from its consequences, and that takes community seriously enough to build actual obligations into its structure rather than settling for the vague fellowship of shared sentiment.

The tradition you have encountered in these pages is not a finished product. It is a reconstruction—honest about its gaps, honest about the distance between the pre-Christian world and our own, honest about the work of interpretation that every practitioner must do. The *Eddas* were written by Christians. The runes were carved by people whose full understanding of them we will never recover. The seasonal rituals have been rebuilt from fragments. Modern Asatru lives in that gap between what was and what can be reconstructed, and the best practitioners understand that gap as a feature rather than a flaw—an invitation to bring genuine thought and genuine practice to a living tradition rather than simply performing a historical reconstruction.

What has not been lost is the structure of values that ran through the original faith. The Norse world understood that a person is defined by their deeds, that fate is real but that how you meet it is your own, that the community you belong to extends backward through the ancestors and forward through the choices you make today, and that the gods are not distant authorities to be appeased but living presences to be known through sustained, honest relationship. These are not ancient ideas made irrelevant by modernity. They are ideas that modernity has made more necessary.

The challenge that every practitioner of Asatru faces is the same challenge the tradition has always set before those who enter it: to live in a way that your life will be worth naming at sumbel, worth honoring at the ancestral altar, worth passing forward as *hamingja* to those who come after you. That challenge does not ask for perfection. It asks for genuine effort, honest self-assessment, and the willingness to return to practice after you have failed at it—which you will, because the tradition is honest enough to know that everyone does.

The gods are still here. The tree still stands. The Norns are still weaving at the base of the well, and every choice you make today is already becoming part of the pattern they are laying down for those who come after you.

That is enough reason to begin. And it is enough reason to continue.

Glossary

The terms collected here span the full range of Asatru's living vocabulary—from the objects used in ritual to the theological concepts that underpin the tradition's understanding of the cosmos, the self, and the relationship between the living and the dead. Some of these words appear throughout the book; others are introduced here for the first time as reference material for deeper practice.

The glossary is organized into three sections: *Ritual Practice*, covering the objects, spaces, and ceremonial acts of Heathen worship; *Key Concepts*, covering the theological, cosmological, and ethical ideas that structure the tradition; and *Community and Tradition*, covering the social forms, historical sources, and organizational structures of modern Asatru. Within each section, entries are arranged alphabetically.

Old Norse spellings are given where they add useful context. Modern English equivalents are provided where they exist. Where a term has been used differently across traditions or time periods, that variation is noted.

Part One: Ritual Practice

The objects, spaces, and ceremonial acts through which Asatru practitioners engage with the divine, the ancestors, and the land.

Alu

An Old Norse formula found in early runic inscriptions, typically interpreted as an invocation of divine protection or magical power rather than a reference to ale or drink, despite the similar sound. Its precise meaning remains debated among scholars, but its consistent appearance in protective and consecrative contexts suggests a function similar to a blessing formula—a spoken or carved declaration that invokes sacred force. Some modern practitioners use *alu* as a closing word for runic workings or inscriptions, in the same way that other traditions use *amen* or *so mote it be.*

Blót

The central ritual act of Asatru worship, in which offerings are made to the gods, ancestors, or land spirits. The Old Norse root carries connotations of both sacrifice and hallowing—the act of giving something over to the sacred while simultaneously consecrating the givers through their participation in the exchange. Historically, blóts involved animal sacrifice, with the blood used to consecrate participants and altar; modern practice typically substitutes mead, ale, juice, or other offerings while maintaining the essential three-part structure of hallowing, sharing, and libation. A blót can be performed alone at a home altar in a matter of minutes or elaborated into a full community ceremony lasting several hours. The underlying principle remains consistent across both scales: the gift relationship between the human community and the divine is renewed, and the sacred connection between the practitioner, the gods, and the earth is reaffirmed. See also: *Hlaut, Hlautbolli, Drekkjarhorn, Sumbel.*

Drekkjarhorn *(also Drekkjarhorn, Drekk(ja)rhorn)*

The drinking horn used to carry the consecrated offering liquid—typically mead or ale—during a blót or sumbel. Traditionally made from the horn of cattle or sheep, hollowed and fitted with a stand since a horn cannot be set down flat, the drekkjarhorn serves as the vessel through which the offering passes from the officiant to the assembled community and finally to the earth as libation. The horn is understood to carry the blessing of the deity invoked during consecration, so that each participant who drinks from it receives that blessing directly. Many kindreds maintain a dedicated drekkjarhorn for ritual use, separate from any horn used for ordinary drinking. The horn is also blown as a call signal to indicate that a ritual is about to begin—in this function it is sometimes called a *moot horn*.

Erfiöl

The memorial ale drunk in the days following a funeral—a ritual drinking ceremony through which the community formally acknowledges the death, honors the deeds of the deceased, and begins the process of integrating their memory into the community's ongoing life. The *erfiöl* is among the oldest documented Norse funeral customs, mentioned in several sagas and law codes. In modern Heathen practice it typically takes the form of a sumbel held in the deceased's honor, with toasts dedicated to their deeds, their name, and their transition into the community of ancestors.

Galdr

The magical practice of chanting or intoning runic names and sacred formulas, understood in the Norse tradition as a means of invoking and directing the forces encoded in those sounds. Where *seiðr* operates primarily through altered states and spirit-travel, galdr is more explicitly verbal—the power resides in the sound itself, in the resonance of the rune's name with the cosmic force it represents. Practitioners intone rune names singly or in combination, sometimes for extended periods, to shift their own state of consciousness, to consecrate objects or spaces, or to invoke specific qualities in a ritual context. Galdr is among the most accessible forms of Norse magical practice for beginners, requiring no specialized equipment—only knowledge of the runes and the willingness to work with sound deliberately.

Gandr

A staff or wand used in Asatru ritual and magical practice, serving as an instrument for channeling and directing sacred force. The *völva*—the Norse seeress—is consistently depicted in the primary sources as carrying a staff, and the gandr appears to have been closely associated with *seiðr* practice, serving both as a practical tool and as a symbol of the practitioner's authority and spiritual capacity. In modern use, a gandr may be carved from a single piece of wood, sometimes marked with runes or symbols relevant to the practitioner's work. It is used to trace symbols in the air during ritual, to direct intention, and to mark the boundaries of sacred space.

Hammarsettung *(Hammer Hallowing)*

The ritual act of consecrating a sacred space by tracing the sign of Mjölnir—Thor's hammer—in each of the four cardinal directions and then upward and downward, establishing a six-directional boundary of protection around the ritual area. The spoken formula most commonly associated with this act is the Old Norse *Hamarr, helga vé þetta ok hindra alla illska*—"Hammer, hallow this sacred space and hinder all harmful things." The Hammarsettung is performed at the beginning of most Asatru rituals, functioning as the opening act that distinguishes the consecrated space from the ordinary world surrounding it. The officiant—typically the *goði* or *gyðja*—faces each direction in turn, tracing the hammer sign while speaking the formula, before completing the hallowing above and below.

Harrow *(also Hörgr)*

An outdoor altar used in Heathen worship, traditionally constructed from piled or stacked stone and placed at a significant natural location—a hilltop, a clearing, the base of a significant tree, a point where two paths cross. The harrow serves as the primary ritual focal point for outdoor blóts and sumbels, a physical threshold between the ordinary world and the sacred one. In modern practice, harrows range from simple cairns of gathered stones to more elaborate permanent constructions. The key requirement is dedication: a harrow that has been formally consecrated and is regularly maintained carries a different quality of sacred presence than a pile of stones assembled for a single occasion.

Hlaut

The consecrated liquid used to bless participants, objects, and sacred spaces during a blót. Historically, *hlaut* referred specifically to the blood of the sacrificed animal, caught in the *hlautbolli* and sprinkled using a branch of evergreen; in modern practice it is the consecrated mead or other offering liquid that has been blessed by the deity invoked and is now understood to carry that divine presence. The sprinkling of hlaut—distributed using the *hlautteinn* across the altar, the assembled participants, and sometimes the surrounding space—is the act through which the blessing of the blót is physically distributed. It is not merely symbolic gesture but an understood mechanism: the consecrated liquid carries the force of the divine contact that the ritual has established.

Hlautbolli *(also Bolli)*

The consecration bowl into which the hlaut is poured following the communal drinking of the horn, and from which it is subsequently sprinkled. The hlautbolli serves as the collecting vessel for what has been blessed—the receptacle that holds the divine presence between the moment of consecration and the moment of distribution. In modern practice, the hlautbolli is often a simple wooden or ceramic bowl designated for ritual use, maintained as a dedicated ritual object and not used for ordinary purposes.

Hlautteinn *(also Teinn)*

The sprig of evergreen—typically yew, fir, or another coniferous branch—used to sprinkle the hlaut during a blót. The hlautteinn is dipped into the hlautbolli and used to distribute the consecrated liquid across the altar, the participants, and the surrounding space in a gesture of blessing and purification. In the original practice, the evergreen was returned to its source after the ritual—placed back beneath the tree or shrub from which it came, along with a small portion of the consecrated liquid, as an acknowledgment of the plant's participation in the rite. Modern practitioners who gather their own hlautteinn typically maintain this custom.

Hof

A dedicated communal hall or building used for Asatru worship—the Norse equivalent of a temple or church, though without the institutional connotations those words carry in modern usage. A hof is a space set apart for regular ritual use by a kindred or community, consecrated for that purpose and maintained as a permanent sacred space. In the Viking Age, hofs were substantial wooden buildings, sometimes housing figures of the gods and serving as centers of community religious life for a region. In modern Asatru, a hof may be a purpose-built structure, a rented hall used regularly by a kindred, or a dedicated room within a private home. What makes a space a hof is not its architecture but its consistent dedication and maintenance as a place of regular worship.

Hörgr

A personal or private altar—the indoor or small-scale counterpart to the harrow. The hörgr is the practitioner's primary physical interface with the sacred in their daily life: a dedicated space within the home where offerings are made, names are spoken, and the ongoing relationship with the gods, ancestors, and land spirits is maintained through regular attention. A hörgr can be as simple as a shelf or windowsill set with significant objects—a representation of a deity, a candle, a horn or cup for offerings, objects belonging to honored ancestors—or as elaborate as a fully constructed altar with carved figures and dedicated ritual tools. The key requirement, as with the harrow, is dedication: the hörgr must be genuinely set apart, regularly tended, and understood as a threshold rather than a display.

Horn (Moot Horn)

A cow's horn adapted for use as a signal instrument by cutting the pointed end and drilling a hole, producing a blowing horn used to call the community together before a ritual begins. The sound of the horn marks the transition from ordinary time to ritual time, announcing that the blót, sumbel, or other ceremony is about to commence. Many kindreds maintain a dedicated moot horn for this purpose. The same animal's second horn is typically used as the drekkjarhorn—the vessel from which offerings are drunk—completing a pair of complementary ritual uses from a single source.

Knésetja *(Knee-Setting)*

The traditional heathen naming ceremony for newborns, in which the child is placed on the knee of the father or a designated elder and formally given a name and family history before the assembled community. The naming is the act through which the child enters the family line and receives their first connection to the ancestral *hamingja*—an unnamed child exists outside the web of communal obligation and sacred identity. In pre-Christian Scandinavia, a child was not considered a full member of the community until named, typically at a gathering of the *Thing*. Modern Heathen families adapt this ceremony in various ways, sometimes incorporating offerings to the Norns in acknowledgment of the fate-threads being woven at the moment of naming.

Mead

Fermented honey wine, the traditional offering liquid of Asatru ritual and the primary substance used in blót and sumbel. Mead occupies a special place in the Norse mythological imagination—the Mead of Poetry, created from the blood of Kvasir and honey, is the source of all inspired speech, and the gods feast on mead in Valhalla. In ritual practice, mead is preferred over other offerings for its mythological associations, its ancient use in the tradition, and its quality as something genuinely produced through effort and time—a fitting gift for the gods. Those who do not drink alcohol may substitute juice or water, or may simply touch their lips to the horn in acknowledgment of the communal sharing without drinking.

Nornagraut

*(Norn Porridge)*A traditional offering of porridge made for the Norns—the three fate-weavers who attend every birth to begin weaving the new child's fate—given in thanks for the safe delivery of a child and in petition for a favorable destiny. The custom is documented in Danish, Faroese, and Norwegian

folk tradition and is among the oldest birth-related religious practices that survived the Christian conversion in folk memory. In modern Heathen practice, nornagraut is typically made and shared by the women of the family or kindred at a birth celebration, with a portion set aside as an offering to the Norns and left at the threshold or beneath a tree.

Oath Ring

A ring—typically of silver or iron—on which sacred oaths are sworn in Asatru ritual. The oath ring is among the most significant objects in the tradition's ritual vocabulary: to swear on the ring is to make a commitment not merely before the assembled community but before the gods themselves, witnessed by forces that will hold the oath-taker to what they have declared. Oath rings appear throughout the sagas as objects of tremendous sacred weight—temple oath rings were kept at cult sites and touched during every formal vow. In modern practice, the kindred's oath ring is brought out at Profession ceremonies, at sumbel when particularly weighty vows are made, and at marriages. Breaking an oath sworn on the ring is among the most serious transgressions the tradition recognizes.

Profession

The ritual act by which a person formally dedicates themselves to Asatru and declares their commitment to the gods, the values, and the community of the tradition. Profession is not an initiation in the esoteric sense—it confers no secret knowledge and grants no special status. It is precisely what its name suggests: a public declaration, made before the assembled kindred and before the gods, that the practitioner chooses this path freely and pledges their faithfulness to it. The ceremony is brief—an oath spoken over the oath ring in the presence of the officiant and the community—but its weight is considerable, as all oaths in the Norse tradition are. Profession should not be undertaken without genuine reflection; it should not be undertaken under social pressure; and no one is required to profess in order to participate in Asatru practice.

Recel *(Incense)*

From the Anglo-Saxon word meaning "to smoke," cognate with the modern English "reek" and the Icelandic place name Reykjavík ("smoky bay"). Incense is used in some Asatru traditions for the purification and preparation of sacred space before ritual, the officiant moving through the space with a burning bundle or incense vessel—the *recelspot* or incense burner—allowing the smoke to clear and consecrate the area. The use of fragrant smoke in Germanic religious practice is documented archaeologically and in several saga references. The specific herbs and resins used vary by tradition and region; juniper, mugwort, and pine resin are among the most commonly referenced in Northern European practice.

Seiðr

The primary Norse magical practice, involving the use of an altered state of consciousness—a trance—to travel in spirit through the Nine Worlds for purposes of divination, healing, fate-working, or communication with gods and ancestors. *Seiðr* was historically the province of the *völva*—the professional seeress who traveled between communities offering her services—and was associated with Freya, who taught it to Óðinn. The practice involves a ritual structure including an elevated seat, the chanting of *varðlokur* (spirit-calling songs) by a supporting group, and the seer's journey in spirit while the body remains in trance. Modern seiðr practice has been reconstructed from primary source accounts, particularly the *Saga of Erik the Red*, and is practiced within contemporary Heathen communities by trained practitioners. See also: *Völva, Varðlokur.*

Stalli

An interior altar dedicated to Heathen worship—used synonymously with *hörgr* in some traditions, though *stalli* tends to refer more specifically to the altar surface itself rather than the broader sacred space it anchors. A stalli may be a dedicated table, a shelf, or a constructed altar at which ritual objects are kept and offerings are made. The term appears in the sagas in descriptions of indoor cult practice, where figures of the gods were kept on a stalli and attended with regular offerings.

Sumbel

A sacred drinking ceremony in which a horn of mead is passed among seated participants, each of whom offers a toast, tells a story, recites a poem, or makes a boast or vow when the horn reaches them. The sumbel is among the most socially and spiritually significant of Asatru's communal practices—not primarily a religious ceremony in the formal sense but a ritual context in which the bonds of the community are renewed, the ancestors are honored, and individual commitments are made before witnesses who will hold the speaker to what they have declared. Words spoken at sumbel over the horn are understood to enter the web of *wyrd* and become part of the pattern of what unfolds—a boast made at sumbel is a commitment, not merely an aspiration. The standard three-round format honors the gods in the first round, ancestors and heroes in the second, and allows personal toasts, stories, and vows in the third. See also: *Drekkjarhorn, Blót*.

Útiseta *(Sitting Out)*

The practice of going to a significant ancestral or sacred location—particularly a burial mound, a crossroads, or a place associated with the land spirits—and remaining there in meditation or light trance, open to whatever communication or impression comes from the dead, the gods, or the forces of the place itself. *Útiseta* appears in several sagas as a recognized practice for receiving guidance, particularly from ancestors, and shares structural features with shamanic practices found across northern Eurasia. Modern practitioners approach it with varying degrees of literalism, but the core practice—deliberate, physically located attention to sacred presence—remains active in contemporary Heathenry, particularly in connection with ancestor work and *seiðr* practice.

Varðlokur

The spirit-calling songs sung by the supporting group during a *seiðr* working to call the relevant spirits and maintain the ritual container while the seer travels in trance. The *Saga of Erik the Red* describes the *varðlokur* as essential to the *völva*'s work—without them, the spirits would not come, and the seer's journey could not be accomplished. The songs are understood to function as both an invocation and a protection: calling what is needed while holding the boundary of the ritual space. Modern seiðr practitioners reconstruct varðlokur using fragments from the primary sources, traditional folk melodies, and material developed through contemporary practice.

Vé

A sacred enclosure or space for worship, typically outdoors and smaller than a hof—more intimate and personal in character, though still understood as consecrated ground. The word appears in Old Norse as a general term for any sacred space, and in some compounds designates the specific enclosure within which religious activities took place at a cult site. In modern practice, a vé may be a marked outdoor space where regular offerings are made, a garden area designated for ritual use, or a temporary enclosure established for a specific ceremony through the Hammarsettung.

Wain

An archaic English word for wagon, preserved in Asatru use because of the historical practice—documented in Tacitus's *Germania* and echoed in several Norse sources—of transporting images of the gods through the landscape in a wagon, the wagon's passage understood as a blessing of the land and people it passed through. The Vanir gods in particular are associated with wagon processions: Freyr's cult involved an annual wagon journey with a priestess who blessed the fields, and the goddess Nerthus was similarly described as traveling in a veiled wagon. The wain appears in modern Heathen practice primarily as a reference point for understanding the itinerant quality of some pre-Christian cultic activity, and occasionally in ritual contexts that recreate or honor that tradition.

Part Two: Key Concepts

The theological, cosmological, and ethical ideas that structure the Asatru understanding of the cosmos, the self, and the relationship between living and divine.

Æsir

The principal family of Norse gods, headed by Óðinn and including Thor, Frigg, Tyr, Heimdallr, Baldr, Bragi, and others. The Æsir are gods of sovereignty, war, wisdom, and social order—their world, Ásgarðr, is characterized by hierarchy, law, and the structures that make civilization possible. The name is the plural of *áss*, meaning "god," and gives Asatru its name: *ása-trú*, faith in the Æsir. The Æsir coexist in the mythology with the Vanir, the second family of Norse gods, following the resolution of the Æsir-Vanir War. Both groups are honored in modern Asatru practice, though the Æsir tend to be more prominent in the surviving primary sources. See also: *Vanir*.

Argr *(also Ergi)*

An Old Norse term denoting unmanliness, effeminacy, or the transgression of gender norms—one of the most serious social insults available in the Viking Age. The accusation of *argr* carried specific legal weight in some contexts: a man so accused could, under certain law codes, challenge the accuser to a duel. The concept is relevant to understanding the Norse magical tradition because male practitioners of *seiðr*—including Óðinn himself—were vulnerable to this accusation, given the art's association with weaving and feminine roles. The fact that the most powerful god in the Norse pantheon practiced an art considered *argr* suggests a tradition that was simultaneously aware of these social categories and willing to transcend them in the pursuit of power and knowledge. See also: *Seiðr*.

Dísir

Female ancestral spirits—the accumulated feminine spiritual power of a family line, understood as watching over and actively protecting the living members of their lineage. The *dísir* are neither fully human nor fully divine but occupy an intermediate position: the honored dead women of a family who retain their connection to and concern for those they have left behind. They are particularly associated with birth, fate, and the welfare of the household, and are honored at the *Dísablót* (Disting) and at Winter Nights. The *dísir* can be benevolent and protective when properly acknowledged or actively harmful when neglected or disrespected—their favor is maintained through regular offerings and the practice of speaking their names. See also: *Disting, Ancestor Veneration.*

Dómr

The reputation or legacy that a person leaves behind at death—the sum of their deeds as remembered and spoken by the community. *Dómr* is among the most important concepts in Asatru's ethical framework because it represents the only form of genuine immortality the tradition recognizes as available to all practitioners, regardless of how they die. The *Hávamál* states it directly: cattle die, kinsmen die, the self must die, but the glory of a good reputation never dies. A person's *dómr* is not their public image during their lifetime but the true account of their character as it becomes clear after death—fixed, unalterable, and permanently part of the web of *wyrd*. See also: *Wyrd, Hamingja.*

Draugr

A restless dead—a person who has died but whose spirit cannot settle, returning to the physical world in a destructive and often monstrous form. The *draugr* represents the dark inversion of the honored ancestor: where the properly mourned and remembered dead bless the land and the living, the neglected or dishonored dead become dangerous. The sagas describe draugar as possessing superhuman strength, the ability to grow to enormous size, and the capacity for deliberate cruelty. They were understood to arise from deaths that were badly managed—through violence, dishonor, improper burial, or an obsessive attachment to possessions—and could be stopped through exhumation, decapitation, and cremation of the remains. The concept reflects the Norse understanding that the relationship between the living and the dead carries genuine obligations on both sides. See also: *Ancestor Veneration, Hamingja*.

Fylgja

One of the semi-independent aspects of the Norse self—the fetch or follower, a spiritual companion that accompanies a person through their life and is connected to their deeper fate. The *fylgja* is sometimes visible to those with second sight, often appearing in animal form that reflects the character of the person it accompanies. It can travel independently of the body, particularly during sleep or trance, and its appearance to others—especially in dreams—is often understood as a harbinger of significant events in the person it follows. At death, the *fylgja* may pass to a descendant, carrying forward some essential quality of the deceased into the next generation. Óðinn's ravens Huginn and Muninn are sometimes understood as divine analogues of the *fylgja*—extensions of his consciousness that travel independently and return with what they have gathered. See also: *Hamr, Hugr, Hamingja*.

Frith *(Old Norse: Friþ)*

The peace, goodwill, and active solidarity that exists within a community—particularly within a kindred or family group. *Frith* is not simply the absence of conflict but a positive quality of relationship: the willingness to support, protect, and remain loyal to those within your circle of obligation, and to hold the bonds of community above personal convenience. Maintaining frith within a kindred is understood as both a social and a cosmological responsibility—because the web of *wyrd* connects all things, the quality of relationships within a community affects the fate of everyone in it. The violation of frith—through betrayal, broken oaths, or the sowing of discord within the group—is among the most serious transgressions the tradition recognizes. See also: *Wyrd, Níð*.

Hamingja

The accumulated luck, spiritual force, and inherited power generated by honorable living—understood in the Norse tradition as a genuine substance that flows through a family line, transmitted from ancestor to descendant and augmented or diminished by the quality of each generation's choices. *Hamingja* is not luck in the sense of random fortune but something closer to a spiritual inheritance: the sum of all the honorable deeds, kept oaths, and genuine relationships built by everyone who has come before you in your lineage. A person of strong hamingja moves through the world with an advantage that is real and transmissible; a person who has squandered or actively damaged their hamingja through dishonor leaves a diminished inheritance for those who follow. Ancestor veneration is in part a practice of maintaining connection with the hamingja stored in the ancestral line. See also: *Dómr, Fylgja, Wyrd.*

Hamr

The shape, appearance, and outer form through which a person presents themselves to the world—one of the four semi-independent aspects of the Norse self. The *hamr* includes not just the physical body but the social persona, the way a person carries themselves, and the impression they make on others. Skilled practitioners of *seiðr* were understood to be able to alter their *hamr*, projecting it at a distance or assuming the form of animals—a practice called *hamfarir* or shape-shifting. At death, the hamr is left behind with the body, returning to the earth. The compound *berserker* derives from the concept of warriors who were said to take on the *hamr* of bears in battle. See also: *Hugr, Fylgja, Hamingja.*

Hugr

The mind, will, and seat of conscious agency—the aspect of the Norse self most closely corresponding to what modern people mean by consciousness or personality. The *hugr* is the driving force of action and intention, the part of the self that makes choices and feels their weight. It can be projected at a distance through intense concentration—the Norse understood that a sufficiently powerful *hugr* could affect people and events far away—and its state is reflected in a person's bearing and presence. When the hugr is strong, a person carries themselves with conviction and presence; when it is depleted or disordered, that weakness is visible. At death, the hugr departs the body, though the precise nature of its subsequent fate varies across sources. See also: *Hamr, Fylgja, Hamingja.*

Jötnar *(singular: Jötunn)*

The giants of Norse mythology—ancient beings who predate the gods and represent the primordial forces of chaos, dissolution, and the untamed aspects of reality. The word derives from a Proto-Germanic root meaning "devourer," reflecting their cosmological function as forces that consume and break down order. The Jötnar are not simply villains: they are complex beings, many of whom are wise, beautiful, and in ongoing relationship with the gods. Óðinn's mother was a giantess; Thor's mother was a giantess; Freyr gave up his sword for the love of the giantess Gerðr. The boundary between gods and giants is consistently blurred in the mythology, reflecting the Norse understanding that chaos and order are not opposites but interdependent forces, each requiring the other. At Ragnarök, the Jötnar will breach Ásgarðr and bring about the destruction of the current world order—but the world that rises from the wreckage will be better than what was destroyed. See also: *Ragnarök, Æsir.*

Landvættir

The land spirits—beings who inhabit specific features of the physical landscape and exert significant influence over the welfare of those who live and work within their territory. Landvættir are not abstract forces but presences with personalities, preferences, and the capacity for both blessing and harm. Pre-Christian Icelandic law required ships approaching the coast to remove their dragon-head prows to avoid frightening the landvættir of the shore. Modern Asatruar maintain relationship with the landvættir of their specific location through regular offerings, respectful behavior on the land, and the conscious acknowledgment that the place they inhabit is already occupied by beings whose goodwill matters. The relationship is reciprocal: the spirits can ensure fertility, safety, and good fortune, or withdraw those gifts if disrespected. See also: *Dísir, Ancestor Veneration.*

Níð

Dishonor—the accumulation of spiritual debt generated by cowardice, oath-breaking, betrayal, and the various forms of conduct that the Norse tradition identified as incompatible with a life of integrity. *Níð* is the opposite of *hamingja*: where hamingja is transmitted forward through honorable living, níð contaminates the lineage and diminishes the possibilities available to those who follow. The Norse tradition took the concept seriously enough to develop specific legal remedies for public accusations of níð—the person so accused could demand satisfaction through combat or formal legal process. In modern Asatru, níð functions as an ethical concept rather than a legal one, but its force remains: the understanding that dishonor is real, that it has consequences beyond the immediate situation, and that its repair requires genuine effort rather than simply moving on. See also: *Hamingja, Dómr, Frith.*

Nornir *(singular: Norn)*

The three female beings who weave the fates of gods and humans at the base of Yggdrasil beside the Well of Urð. Their names—*Urðr* (what has been), *Verðandi* (what is becoming), and *Skuldr* (what shall be)—describe their relationship to time rather than their personalities, and their work is best understood not as the arbitrary assignment of fate but as the ongoing recording and weaving of consequences: every action taken by every being in the Nine Worlds contributes to the pattern they are laying down. The Nornir are not worshipped in the conventional sense—the primary sources suggest no cult addressed to them—but they are acknowledged, honored at birth through offerings of nornagraut, and present in the consciousness of any Asatruar who works seriously with the concept of *wyrd*. See also: *Wyrd, Nornagraut, Hamingja.*

Örlög

The primal law or primordial fate—the accumulated weight of all that has already happened, laid down at the base of *wyrd* before any individual life begins. Where *wyrd* is the ongoing web of fate being woven in the present, *örlög* is the foundation beneath it: the immovable record of what has already occurred, which cannot be changed but which shapes what is possible from this point forward. A person's örlög includes the accumulated deeds and *hamingja* of all their ancestors, the circumstances of their birth, and the pattern established before they had any capacity for choice. Understanding örlög is essential to understanding the Norse conception of responsibility: you did not choose your starting point, but you are fully responsible for what you do with it. See also: *Wyrd, Hamingja, Nornir.*

Ragnarök

The fate of the gods—the mythological event toward which the entire Norse cosmological structure moves, in which the forces of chaos breach the boundaries of order, the gods fall in battle, and the current world is destroyed. Ragnarök is not the end but a transformation: from the destruction, a new world rises—greener and more fertile than the one destroyed—populated by a new generation of gods and the human survivors who sheltered in Yggdrasil's branches. The Norse understanding of Ragnarök is neither purely pessimistic nor falsely optimistic: the gods know they will fall and they choose to fight anyway, not because they expect to win but because the alternative—abandoning the world without defense—is incompatible with honor. For modern Asatruar, Ragnarök functions as a model for how to inhabit a world that offers no ultimate guarantees: with clear eyes, genuine commitment, and the willingness to meet what comes without requiring a promise of victory first. See also: *Æsir, Jötnar, Yggdrasil.*

Seiðr

See Part One: Ritual Practice.

Vanir

The second family of Norse gods, associated with fertility, prosperity, magic, and the cycles of the natural world. The principal Vanir are Freyr, Freya, and Njörðr—all of whom came to live among the Æsir following the resolution of the Æsir-Vanir War, becoming honorary members of the Æsir while retaining their distinctive character. Where the Æsir gods tend toward structure, law, and the ordered aspects of existence, the Vanir are more closely associated with the organic rhythms of the earth, with *seiðr* magic, and with a more fluid approach to social and sexual norms. Freya taught *seiðr* to Óðinn himself—an indication of the Vanir's particular mastery of the tradition's most powerful magical practice. Both families are honored in modern Asatru, and the integration of their different approaches to the sacred is understood as one of the tradition's core strengths. See also: *Æsir, Seiðr.*

Völva *(plural: Völur)*

A professional seeress in pre-Christian Norse society—a woman who traveled between communities performing *seiðr* workings, prophesying, and offering magical assistance in exchange for food, shelter, and payment. The *völva* occupied an ambiguous social position: revered for her abilities, sought after for her knowledge, and simultaneously feared for the power she wielded and the transgression her practice represented. She is depicted in the primary sources as carrying a staff, wearing distinctive clothing, and requiring a specific ritual support structure—including the chanting of *varðlokur*—to do her work. The *Völuspá*—the "Prophecy of the Seeress"—is narrated by a *völva* whom Óðinn has woken from the dead to question about the fate of the cosmos. In modern Asatru, practitioners who specialize in *seiðr* work may take on the role and title of *völva*, though the term carries significant historical weight and is not used casually. See also: *Seiðr, Varðlokur.*

Wyrd

The web of fate—the interconnected fabric of cause and consequence that links all beings, all actions, and all times in the Norse cosmos. *Wyrd* is not determinism in the modern sense: it does not mean that everything is fixed in ad-

vance. What it means is that every action has consequences that ripple outward through the web, affecting possibilities for everyone connected to the
actor, and that the accumulated weight of all past actions—*örlög*—shapes
but does not entirely determine what is possible in the present. The Nornir
weave *wyrd* at the base of Yggdrasil, but they do not invent the pattern from
nothing: they record and integrate the consequences of choices already
made. Understanding wyrd is essential to understanding the Norse ethical
framework—because your choices affect not only your own fate but the fate
of everyone whose threads run near yours in the web, the tradition places
genuine weight on the quality of those choices. See also: *Örlög, Nornir,
Hamingja, Dómr.*

Yggdrasil

The World Tree—the immense ash at the center of the Norse cosmos whose
roots reach into the lowest realms and whose branches shelter the highest,
holding the Nine Worlds in relationship with one another. Yggdrasil is the
axis of existence: the structural fact of the cosmos without which the Nine
Worlds would not simply drift apart but cease to exist. Three roots draw
from three sacred wells—the Well of Fate tended by the Nornir, the Well
of Wisdom where Óðinn sacrificed his eye, and Hvergelmir, source of all
rivers, at whose base the serpent Níðhöggr gnaws perpetually. The tree
is simultaneously being consumed and sustained—gnawed from below,
eaten by stags above, tended daily by the Nornir with water and clay. This
paradox is not incidental to the mythology but central to it: the structure
that holds everything together is itself mortal, subject to the same forces
of entropy and dissolution that affect all things. For modern Asatruar, Yggdrasil serves as both cosmological map and meditation object—the image
of an interconnected universe in which every being and every action is part
of a larger pattern. See also: *Nine Worlds, Nornir, Wyrd.*

Part Three: Community and Tradition

The social forms, historical sources, organizational structures, and key figures of modern Asatru practice.

Althing *(Old Norse: Alþing)*

The great assembly—historically, the legislative and judicial gathering of the Icelandic commonwealth, held annually from 930 CE onward at Þingvellir. The Althing was one of the world's earliest parliamentary institutions, and its decision in approximately 1000 CE to officially adopt Christianity—while permitting private pagan practice—marked the formal end of public Norse paganism in Iceland. In modern Asatru, the term *althing* is used by some organizations to describe their annual national gathering, combining the original meaning of a legal and deliberative assembly with the contemporary function of a community meeting, ritual gathering, and shared celebration. The Icelandic national Asatru organization, Ásatrúarfélagið, maintains a formal connection to this tradition.

Ásatrúarfélagið

The Icelandic National Association of Asatru—the organization founded in 1972 by Sveinbjörn Beinteinsson and eleven other Icelanders that formally re-established public worship of the Norse gods in the modern era and sparked the global Asatru revival. Officially recognized as a religious organization by the Icelandic government in 1973, Ásatrúarfélagið is now the largest non-Christian religious organization in Iceland and is legally authorized to officiate at marriages, naming ceremonies, and funerals. Its founding is generally understood as the beginning of the modern Heathen movement. The organization has historically been inclusive and non-folkish in its orientation, welcoming practitioners regardless of ethnic background, and has officiated at ceremonies for practitioners from outside Iceland, including same-sex couples.

Ásatrú Folk Assembly *(AFA)*

One of the largest Asatru organizations in the United States, founded by Stephen McNallen. The AFA takes a folkish position—the view that Asatru is the indigenous spiritual tradition of people of Northern European descent and that ethnic heritage is relevant to practice. This position is contested within the broader Heathen community, with many organizations and practitioners explicitly rejecting it as having no historical basis in actual Norse religious practice, which was defined by cultural participation rather than bloodline. Practitioners researching community affiliation should be aware of this distinction between folkish and universalist approaches to the tradition.

Elder Futhark

The oldest fully formed runic alphabet, used across the Germanic world until approximately 700 CE. The name derives from the first six runes: *Fehu, Uruz, Thurisaz, Ansuz, Raidho, Kenaz*. The Elder Futhark contains twenty-four runes organized into three groups of eight called *ættir* (singular *ætt*), and is the runic system most widely used in modern Asatru practice for both divination and magical work. Approximately 350 inscriptions in the Elder Futhark have been recovered, most on weapons, jewelry, and runestones. Its rune names have been reconstructed through comparison with the later Younger Futhark and the Anglo-Saxon Futhorc, since no contemporary manuscript record of the Elder Futhark names survives. See also: *Younger Futhark, Runes*.

Edda

The collective name for the two primary literary sources of Norse mythology: the *Poetic Edda* and the *Prose Edda*. The *Poetic Edda*—also called the *Elder Edda* or *Sæmundar Edda*—is a collection of anonymous mythological and heroic poems preserved primarily in the thirteenth-century Icelandic manuscript known as the *Codex Regius*, rediscovered in 1643. The *Prose Edda* was written around 1220 CE by the Icelandic chieftain and scholar Snorri Sturluson as a guide to skaldic poetic technique, providing systematic accounts of Norse mythology to explain the kennings and allusions that skaldic poetry employed. Both are indispensable to modern Asatru practice and should be read critically—the *Poetic Edda* because its poems were composed for audiences already familiar with the mythology and assume knowledge the modern reader must reconstruct; the

Prose Edda because Snorri was a Christian writing more than two centuries after Iceland's conversion, and his interpretive framework reflects that distance. See also: *Snorri Sturluson, Hávamál, Völuspá.*

Einherjar

The chosen dead who dwell in Valhalla—warriors selected by the Valkyries from those who fell in battle and brought to Óðinn's hall to feast, fight, and prepare for Ragnarök. The *einherjar* fight each day and are restored to full health each evening; they feast on the boar Sæhrímnir, who is slaughtered and resurrected daily, and drink mead from the goat Heiðrún. They are not in Valhalla as a reward for valor but as conscripts in Óðinn's army, chosen for their martial skill and kept in readiness for the final battle. Their feast day in the modern Heathen calendar falls on November 11th—a date deliberately chosen to coincide with Armistice Day, honoring the overlap between the tradition's reverence for those who died in battle and the modern commemoration of war dead. See also: *Valhalla, Valkyrie, Ragnarök.*

Folkish Heathenry

A strand of modern Heathenry that holds Norse paganism to be the indigenous spiritual tradition of people of Northern European descent and restricts full participation or membership to those of the appropriate ethnic background. Folkish Heathenry has no historical basis in the actual practice of pre-Christian Norse religion, which spread across a vast geographic area through cultural contact and was defined by participation in the tradition's practices rather than by bloodline. Modern scholarship consistently finds no ethnic exclusivity in the historical Norse religious tradition. Many Heathen organizations—including the Troth and Ásatrúarfélagið—explicitly reject folkish positions. Practitioners should be aware that the term "folkish" is used consistently within the community to denote ethnic exclusivity, and that groups using this descriptor may hold positions incompatible with the tradition's actual historical character.

Fulltrúi

A person's primary divine patron—the god or goddess with whom they have developed the deepest and most specific relationship, whose domain most clearly maps onto their life, and whose presence they invoke most regularly in practice. The word means "fully trusted one" and implies a relationship of genuine mutual commitment rather than casual preference. A fulltrúi is not formally assigned or initiated; the relationship develops organically through sustained practice and attention, often announcing itself through recurring resonance with a particular deity's stories, symbols, or qualities. Having a fulltrúi does not preclude honoring other gods—it means one relationship in the divine community has become primary. See also: *Meeting the Gods, Blót.*

Goði *(feminine: Gyðja; plural: Goðar)*

A priest or priestess in Asatru—the person who officiates at blóts, sumbels, and other ritual ceremonies, and who may also serve as a community leader, spiritual counselor, and keeper of the lore within a kindred. The role of *goði* in pre-Christian Iceland carried legal as well as religious authority; the *goðar* were the chieftains of their districts, responsible for maintaining the local cult and representing their community at the Althing. In modern Asatru, the goði's role is primarily liturgical and pastoral—they lead rituals, offer guidance to practitioners, and serve as a point of continuity and knowledge within the kindred. There is no universal ordination process for goðar; recognition of the role varies between traditions and organizations. See also: *Kindred, Althing.*

Hávamál

"Sayings of the High One"—a long didactic poem attributed to Óðinn and preserved in the *Poetic Edda*, containing practical wisdom about daily conduct, advice on relationships and hospitality, an account of how Óðinn won the runes through his nine-day ordeal on Yggdrasil, and a catalog of magical knowledge. The *Hávamál* is the primary ethical text of modern Asatru—the source most frequently cited as a guide to daily life, personal conduct, and the values the tradition holds central. It is not a sacred scripture in the sense of revealed divine law but a collection of hard-won wisdom, addressed to human beings navigating a difficult world, from a god who understands difficulty from the inside. Serious practitioners typically read it slowly, return to it repeatedly across years of practice, and find different things in it at different stages of their development. See also: *Edda, Nine Noble Virtues.*

Heathenry

The broader term used alongside Asatru to describe the modern revival of pre-Christian Norse and Germanic religious practice. Where "Asatru" derives from Old Norse and refers specifically to faith in the Æsir, "Heathenry" is an English term derived from the word *heathen*—originally meaning "those who live on the heath," applied by early Christian missionaries to the rural populations of Northern Europe who were slowest to convert. Modern practitioners have reclaimed the term, wearing it with the same pride that "pagan" has been reclaimed in other contemporary polytheist traditions. The two terms are largely interchangeable in modern use, though some practitioners prefer one over the other; "Heathenry" tends to be used as the broader category encompassing various reconstructionist approaches to Germanic paganism, while "Asatru" sometimes refers more specifically to the Icelandic-influenced strand of the revival.

Kenning

A compound poetic metaphor characteristic of Old Norse and Anglo-Saxon poetry, in which a concept is described through an evocative paraphrase rather than named directly. Kennings are among the most distinctive features of skaldic poetry and are essential to understanding the primary sources: the sea becomes "the whale's road," gold becomes "the fire of the Rhine," a sword becomes "the wound-snake," poetry becomes "Kvasir's blood." Snorri Sturluson wrote the *Prose Edda* primarily to explain the kennings used in skaldic verse, preserving a systematic account of Norse mythology in the process. Modern readers of the Eddas encounter kennings constantly and must learn to read through them rather than past them—the poetic compression they represent often carries theological weight that literal language would flatten.

Kindred

The primary social and religious unit of modern Asatru—a community of practitioners who gather regularly for ritual practice, seasonal observances, and mutual support. The kindred functions as an extended family in the social sense: a circle of obligation and loyalty within which the values of frith, hospitality, and mutual accountability are actively practiced rather than theoretically held. Kindreds vary enormously in size, structure, and formality, from small groups of friends who meet for seasonal blóts to formally organized communities with elected leadership and established ritual practice. Practitioners who cannot find a local kindred may practice solitarily, but the tradition understands the kindred as the ideal context for Heathen life—many of its most important practices, particularly sumbel and the communal blót, are most fully themselves when shared. See also: *Goði, Frith, Althing.*

Lore

The body of knowledge drawn from the primary sources—the *Eddas*, the sagas, the runic inscriptions, and the secondary scholarship that interprets them—that forms the textual foundation of Asatru practice. In community discussions, "the lore" refers to what the historical and literary sources actually say, as distinguished from individual interpretation, modern innovation, or *UPG* (Unverified Personal Gnosis). The distinction between lore and UPG is one of the most important conceptual tools in modern Heathen discourse, allowing practitioners to communicate clearly about the basis for their claims and practices. Serious engagement with the lore—reading the primary sources directly, studying the scholarship, and maintaining intellectual honesty about what the texts actually say—is understood as a core obligation of practice rather than an optional supplement to it. See also: *Edda, UPG, Hávamál.*

Mjölnir

Thor's hammer—the most powerful weapon in the Norse cosmos, forged by the dwarves Brokkr and Eitri, capable of leveling mountains and returning to Thor's hand after being thrown. Beyond its function as a weapon, Mjölnir served as the instrument of consecration and blessing in pre-Christian Norse practice: it was used to bless newborns, to hallow marriages, to consecrate the dead for their funeral journey, and to mark the boundaries of sacred space. More than fifty Mjölnir pendants have been recovered from Viking Age archaeological sites across Scandinavia and the British Isles, confirming that wearing the hammer as an amulet was a common practice—one that intensified during the Viking Age possibly in response to the growing visibility of the Christian cross. In modern Asatru, Mjölnir is the most widely worn symbol of Heathen identity and remains the primary instrument of ritual consecration through the Hammarsettung. See also: *Hammarsettung, Thor.*

Nine Noble Virtues *(NNV)*

A modern ethical framework for Asatru practice, codified in the 1970s by figures associated with the Odinic Rite in Britain, drawing on themes present throughout the *Eddas* and sagas—particularly the *Hávamál.* The nine virtues are Courage, Truth, Discipline, Fidelity, Honor, Hospitality, Industriousness, Self-Reliance, and Perseverance. The NNV are not ancient—their specific formulation as a list of nine is a modern synthesis—but they are well-grounded in the values that the primary sources consistently present as admirable. They function in modern Heathen practice as a practical ethical guide, a framework for self-assessment, and a statement of communal values rather than as commandments or doctrinal requirements. See also: *Hávamál, Dómr, Hamingja.*

Nine Worlds

The nine realms that make up the Norse cosmos, held in relationship by the roots and branches of Yggdrasil: Ásgarðr (realm of the Æsir), Vanaheimr (realm of the Vanir), Miðgarðr (realm of humanity), Jötunheimr (realm of the giants), Niflheim (primordial realm of ice), Muspelheim (primordial realm of fire), Álfheimr (realm of the light elves), Svartálfaheimr/Niðavellir (realm of the dwarves), and Helheim (realm of the dead). The precise spatial arrangement of the Nine Worlds is not specified in the primary sources and has been the subject of ongoing scholarly discussion. What is consistent across the sources is the understanding that the worlds are real, distinct, and interconnected—that the cosmos is genuinely populated by diverse beings across multiple planes of existence, all held in relationship by the World Tree. See also: *Yggdrasil, Æsir, Jötnar.*

Odinic Rite

A British Asatru organization founded in the early 1970s that played a significant role in the early development of modern Heathenry, including the formulation of the Nine Noble Virtues. The Odinic Rite has maintained a folkish orientation—emphasizing the tradition's connection to Northern European peoples—while also contributing substantially to the development of modern Heathen ritual practice and ethical frameworks. Its influence on the early revival, particularly in Britain and among English-speaking practitioners internationally, makes it a significant historical reference point regardless of the practitioner's position on the folkish question.

Skald

A Norse court poet—a professional composer and performer of complex alliterative verse who served at the courts of kings and chieftains during the Viking Age, composing praise poetry, commemorative verse, and mythological poetry in the demanding skaldic style. The skalds were among the most important transmitters of Norse mythological and historical knowledge, and their poems—preserved in the later sagas and in Snorri's *Prose Edda*—are among the primary sources that modern Asatru draws on. Skaldic poetry is among the most technically demanding literary forms ever developed, characterized by strict metrical rules, extensive use of kennings, and a compressed allusive style that presupposes deep familiarity with the mythological tradition. The god Bragi is the divine patron of skalds. See also: *Kenning, Edda, Hávamál.*

Snorri Sturluson

Icelandic chieftain, historian, and poet (1179–1241), author of the *Prose Edda* and the *Heimskringla* (a history of the Norwegian kings), and one of the most important single figures in the preservation of Norse mythological knowledge. Snorri was a Christian writing approximately two centuries after Iceland's official conversion, and his work must be read with that context in mind—his interpretive framework, his occasional euhemerism (treating the gods as deified human kings), and his rationalizing tendencies all reflect his medieval Christian education as much as the pre-Christian tradition he was documenting. Despite these limitations, without the *Prose Edda* our understanding of Norse mythology would be dramatically thinner, and Snorri's account of the cosmology, the gods, and the mythological narratives remains the most systematic source available. See also: *Edda, Prose Edda, Kenning*.

The Troth

One of the largest and most prominent Asatru organizations in the English-speaking world, founded in 1987 and explicitly committed to an inclusive, non-folkish approach to Heathenry that welcomes practitioners of all ethnic and cultural backgrounds. The Troth publishes *Idunna*, a journal of Heathen scholarship and practice, maintains a clergy training program, and provides a directory of affiliated kindreds and practitioners. Its commitment to diversity and its rejection of racial exclusivity make it a useful reference point for practitioners seeking community that reflects the historical Norse tradition's actual geographic and cultural breadth.

UPG *(Unverified Personal Gnosis)*

A term used in modern Heathen community discussion to designate spiritual insights, impressions, or understandings that a practitioner has developed through personal experience—ritual, meditation, direct encounter with the divine—rather than from the primary sources. UPG is understood as a legitimate and necessary part of living religious practice: the lore does not cover everything, the gods communicate in ways that are not always textually grounded, and the personal dimension of practice must have a vocabulary. At the same time, the distinction between UPG and lore is carefully maintained in serious Heathen discourse—practitioners are expected to be clear about which of their claims are textually supported and which are personal, and to avoid presenting UPG as historical fact. The tension between lore and UPG is understood not as a problem to be resolved but as the productive edge where a living tradition meets its inherited foundation. See also: *Lore, Edda.*

Valkyrie *(Old Norse: Valkyrja, plural: Valkyrjur)*

Óðinn's female choosers of the slain—beings who move through the battlefield selecting which warriors will die and bringing the chosen dead to Valhalla. The modern image of the Valkyrie as a noble, beautiful maiden escorting fallen heroes is historically attested but incomplete: the earlier sources emphasize their role in actively choosing and causing death, weaving the fate of warriors before the battle begins, and functioning as projections of Óðinn's will rather than as compassionate guides. The poem *Darraðarljóð*, preserved in *Njál's Saga*, depicts twelve Valkyries weaving the outcome of the Battle of Clontarf on a loom strung with human entrails—an image far darker than popular representation suggests. In modern Asatru, Valkyries are understood both in their mythological function and as a model of the kind of total commitment—to a purpose, to a cause, to Óðinn's larger project—that the tradition consistently honors. See also: *Einherjar, Valhalla, Óðinn.*

Valhalla *(Old Norse: Valhöll)*

The great hall of Óðinn in Ásgarðr where the *Einherjar*—the chosen slain—dwell, feast, and prepare for Ragnarök. Valhalla is among the most famous concepts in Norse mythology and one of the most frequently misunderstood: it was not the Norse heaven in the sense of a universal reward for the virtuous dead, but a specific military institution—Óðinn's barracks, populated by warriors selected for their martial skill and kept in readiness for the final battle. Entry required dying in battle and being chosen by the Valkyries; most of the dead, regardless of how honorably they had lived, went to Helheim instead. The idealization of Valhalla in popular culture has often obscured the fact that the Norse afterlife was far more varied and nuanced than a simple warrior's paradise. See also: *Einherjar, Valkyrie, Helheim.*

Völuspá

"The Prophecy of the Seeress"—the opening poem of the *Poetic Edda* and one of the most important texts in the Norse tradition. Narrated by a *völva* whom Óðinn has woken from the dead to question, the *Völuspá* describes the creation of the cosmos, the age of the gods, the death of Baldr, the binding of Loki, and the events of Ragnarök—ending with the vision of the new world rising from the sea after the destruction of the old. The poem is dense, allusive, and deliberately oracular in tone, addressed to an audience already familiar with the mythological tradition and requiring significant scholarly apparatus for the modern reader. It is nevertheless essential reading for anyone serious about Asatru, both for its cosmological content and for the model of prophetic speech it embodies—the *völva* speaking to power with total clarity about what is coming, regardless of whether the listener wants to hear it. See also: *Edda*, *Völva*, *Ragnarök*.

Younger Futhark

The runic alphabet that developed from the Elder Futhark around 750–800 CE and became the primary writing system of the Viking Age in Scandinavia. The Younger Futhark reduced the Elder Futhark's twenty-four runes to sixteen—paradoxically, fewer runes at the same time as the language was becoming more complex—and introduced significant variation in runic forms across different regions. It is the system in which the vast majority of Viking Age runestones are inscribed and represents the living runic tradition of the historical Norse peoples. While the Elder Futhark is more widely used in modern Asatru magical practice, knowledge of the Younger Futhark is essential for reading the primary runestone inscriptions that constitute some of the most direct evidence of pre-Christian Norse religious practice. See also: *Elder Futhark*, *Runes*.

References

The sources listed here represent the essential starting library for any serious student of Asatru—primary texts that form the foundation of the tradition, scholarly works that place them in historical and cultural context, and practical guides for those building a living practice. This is not an exhaustive bibliography but a curated point of entry: the books and resources most likely to reward sustained engagement over years of study.

Primary Sources

The Poetic Edda – Translated by Carolyne Larrington. Oxford University Press, 2014. The most reliable modern English translation of the *Codex Regius*, with useful notes and introduction.

The Prose Edda – Snorri Sturluson. Translated by Jesse Byock. Penguin Classics, 2005. Accessible translation with a clear introduction to Snorri's context and method.

Hávamál – Available in multiple translations. The edition by W.H. Auden and Paul B. Taylor (*Norse Poems*, Athlone Press, 1981) preserves the poem's rhythmic quality; Jackson Crawford's translation (2019) prioritizes clarity for modern readers.

The Sagas of Icelanders – Edited by Örnólfur Thorsson. Penguin Classics, 2000. A comprehensive single-volume anthology including *Egils saga*, *Njáls* *saga*, *Laxdæla saga*, and others essential to understanding Norse religious practice in daily life.

Secondary Sources

Our Troth (2 volumes) – The Troth. 3rd edition, 2022. The most comprehensive reference work on modern Asatru practice, covering history, theology, ritual, and the individual gods in depth.

Norse Mythology: A Guide to the Gods, Heroes, Rituals, and Beliefs – John Lindow. Oxford University Press, 2001. Rigorous scholarly encyclopedia of Norse mythological figures and concepts, organized alphabetically.

The Viking Spirit: An Introduction to Norse Mythology and Religion – Daniel McCoy. CreateSpace, 2016. Accessible scholarly introduction to Norse religion, drawing on primary sources throughout. McCoy's website NorseMythology.org is also an excellent ongoing reference.

Gods and Myths of Northern Europe – H.R. Ellis Davidson. Penguin Books, 1964. A foundational work of Norse religious scholarship, still valuable for its synthesis of mythological and archaeological evidence.

The Norse Myths: A Guide to the Gods and Heroes – Carolyne Larrington. Thames & Hudson, 2017. A scholarly but accessible survey of the mythological tradition, with attention to how the myths function as a system.

A Practical Heathen's Guide to Asatru – Patricia Lafayllve. Llewellyn Publications, 2013. One of the most useful practical introductions to modern Heathen practice for beginners.

Online Resources

NorseMythology.org — Daniel McCoy's rigorously sourced reference site on Norse mythology and religion.

The Troth — thetroth.org — Resources, kindred finder, and publications from one of the largest inclusive Heathen organizations.

Ásatrúarfélagið — asatru.is — The Icelandic national organization; provides context for the tradition's living center.

Youtube

Ocean Keltoi
A well-respected channel that covers various topics related to Norse Paganism, Heathenry, and Asatru.
https://www.youtube.com/c/OceanKeltoi

The Wisdom of Odin
Focuses on personal experiences and teachings within Norse Paganism, sharing rituals, insights, and discussions.
https://www.youtube.com/c/TheWisdomofOdin

Midgard Musings
A Heathen-focused channel that shares information about modern Asatru practice, rituals, and spiritual guidance.
https://www.youtube.com/c/MidgardMusings

Jackson Crawford
An expert on Old Norse language and literature, providing academic insights into Norse mythology and culture.
https://www.youtube.com/c/JacksonCrawford